Small Moments

A Child's Memories of the Civil Rights Movement

Mary M. Barrow

Small Moments: A Child's Memories of the Civil Rights Movement
© copyright 2014 by Mary M. Barrow.

ISBN 13: 978-1-940014-06-7

Library of Congress Catalog Number: 2013954615

Printed in the United States of America

First Printing: 2014

17 16 15 14 13 5 4 3 2 1

Cover and interior design by Laura Drew.

Wise Ink Creative Publishing
53 Oliver Ave S
Minneapolis, MN 55405
www.wiseinkpub.com

To order, visit www.itascabooks.com or call 1-800-901-3480.
Reseller discounts available.

In memory of

Amelia MacIntosh

1902–1964

Contents

While the first Freedom Ride was organized in 1947 to protest segregation in interstate travel, African American passengers were still banned from the berths and dining cars on Pullman trains throughout the U.S. in 1959. Segregated passenger cars were the norm.

During those same years, "defacto segregation," or segregation by choice, increased as African Americans arrived in the Northeast from the South in search of jobs and whites left the Northeastern industrial cities. This period is often referred to as the Second Great Migration.

Moving With Amelia

(August, 1959)

WHEN SHE WALKED, Amelia's hips pumped up and down, gracing me with comfort. Such comfort I knew was unfair as her weight was painful. Yet watching the movement in the enormous roundness of her hips—solid and pliable like the mounds of dough she kneaded and let rise on the kitchen counter—created a feeling like sitting in the cherished warmth of a mother's lap.

Amelia was Southern and very dark brown. She wore heavy-rimmed glasses that sat on her puffed-out cheeks rather than on her nose. Her carefully polished lace-up shoes were stretched in the toes and frayed along the edges where her ankles swelled over the tops, and they smelled like bakers' yeast—slightly sour but also sweet. And when she took moments to rest, Amelia sat with a great grunt, her enormous weight flattening out her bottom, challenging me to be patient so that the warmth within her could expand against her "crust," the toughness

1

she needed to survive. She would then reach for me, or my brother, Chuck, pull us to her, and allow us to sit cuddled close beneath her arms.

I called her Mimi.

All my memories of Mimi include her size. There were also memories of days, like our first in New Jersey, when she was panting, sweat dripping down her face while she was clearly thwarted by her volume. That day, my skinny little five-year-old white hand was tightly clutched in hers as she pulled me along the platform at the Trenton Railway Station. We'd just arrived at the station, and it felt good to be off the train, to feel my legs carry me without swaying or bumping into the rough velveteen seats along the passenger car aisles. I remember standing still for a moment, hoping to rid myself of the feeling of movement, when Amelia yanked me forward and I stumbled to alertness. Clearly, there was no time to pause. She was frantic. If she didn't find help, the train would leave with our suitcases.

The other passengers rushed by, and Amelia's weight seemed to swell with her consternation, which had the counter effect of slowing her down. Her grip on my hand tightened and I felt the tug of her tension. On the other side of her broad hips, I knew she fiercely squeezed my little brother's even smaller fingers because he started crying.

"*Oh Lord*," I thought, imitating a tone of frustration my mother often used. Mama hated when we made a commotion in public, especially if Amelia was involved, so like Mama, I looked to see if anyone had noticed, and plastered on a smile. But oddly, unlike back home in Chattanooga, Tennessee, not one person slowed or even glanced in our direction despite Chuck's tears. And Amelia wasn't in the mood to take notice of that, either.

"Hush, child. I can't be fooling with you right now," she snapped at Chuck without looking at him. "I gots to get our belongings." And since Chuck was her favorite—the one she never ignored—I knew she meant business.

"But Mimi," Chuck pleaded, his chubby, baby-fat legs dancing like maybe he had to pee, *again.*

"Hush now." Amelia leaned forward, looked up and down the platform as if such a stance would help her vision. Her huge breasts pushed the front of her cotton dress out like wind-stretched sails, blocking my view. Chuck pulled backward to look at me behind her skirt and gave me a pleading "help me" expression he'd perfected to get his own way, but there wasn't anything I could do except shrug my shoulders and stick my tongue out at him. Amelia yanked both our hands.

Steam whooshed up around us in a thick cloud, smelling like burned metal and grease. Our cotton shirts, already dirty from two days of travel, stuck to us while beads of sweat nearly as big as Chuck's tears dripped down Amelia's forehead. In August, the humidity in New Jersey was worse than the heat, and despite being only mid-morning and nowhere near time for lunch, the thought of an afternoon swim became as overpowering as an urge to itch day-old chiggers.

"Can we go to the lake, Mimi?" I asked.

Amelia inhaled deeply and puffed herself up like she knew she'd start shrinking when she answered. "You lost your mind or something? You seen any lake? Ain't no lake here. We ain't back there on the mountain no more, and there ain't nothing here like back there. Now don't be talking your foolishness."

Her words, despite the endless weeks of preparation, seemed to slap me awake. Details suddenly became clear and I decided to memorize everything, as if in doing so I could more quickly find the similarities that would make it feel like home.

Many of the other passengers had already moved past us when the engine of the train began rumbling loudly, then hissing and letting out a belch of steam. "Lord, have mercy," Amelia muttered, pulling us away from the rising cloud of wetness. When the air cleared, we were only a few feet farther down the platform, but the whole world had changed. Amelia was right. Nothing here was like back there. There was litter along the rails in front of the flat grate of the engine, and globs of melting gum on the concrete. The sun glared. No one greeted anyone and no one smiled. The two ladies walking quickly next to two men in seersucker jackets didn't wear white cotton gloves, like my mother, nor did they have on broad-rimmed hats to protect their skin. My daddy would have said they were women, not ladies, reminding me there is a difference. And there were two girls about my age wearing Bermuda shorts and ankle socks with scuffed shoes, like they were playing in the yard instead of out in public. I looked up at Amelia to get her reaction, noticed those big beads of sweat were streaming down under her eyes, and decided it wasn't a good time to ask any more questions.

She glanced down at me, then turned away and wiped her cheek on her shoulder. She moved us toward a boy in a porter's uniform sitting lazily on a stack of tied-up magazines behind the newspaper stand. "Can't you help me, boy?" she shouted in a tone she normally reserved for children who back-talked her.

The boy jumped. Got my attention, too. Amelia was getting mad. That's what she did when things got to be too much. She stoked herself up and got mad. Fought, if she had to.

"Yes'm, I can help you," the boy answered, like he'd had experience with her already.

"Aright then. Mr. Bill, man I work for, was supposed to meet me here, but he ain't here and I got to get these chil'en—"

That boy moved fast, right past her, pulled his trolley through the steam and up next to the door of the passenger car. "Where your cases, lady? This train sure as hell ain't gonna sit here all day."

I thought Amelia would wallop him one on the side of the head for talking like that, interrupting and being rude, and using that *h*-word. She'd walloped Peter, her husband, for saying that word in front of us children, and clear as day she wouldn't put up with some young'un saying it. So it surprised me when all she did was yank me and Chuck off to the side. "That's them," she said nodding toward the stack of suitcases and cardboard boxes shoved up behind a metal chain at the end of the Pullman car.

"Get out of the way so I can throw them off," the boy shouted. "This train is gonna move in a minute." He was small but strong as an ox, and he pulled everything—suitcases, boxes, even an old sea trunk—down like none of it weighed more than a pound and shoved it all out the door.

The hard leather suitcases were the first to land, followed by four large cardboard boxes that looked like they'd burst open. Amelia had wrapped white cotton rope end to end and crossways around those boxes, but the bottoms sagged and the sides were crushed. Three or four of them were as big as small coffins so the boy had to drag them off the train, which was a struggle as the ropes snagged on the edges of the stairs. He pushed and pulled until finally a conductor set down his ticket case and helped him. Together, the boy and the conductor barely managed to get the rest of our belongings onto the platform before the whole line of passenger cars jerked and shuttered.

"Pretty damn close, lady," the boy said.

Amelia nodded. She had not released our hands. My wrist ached in response as Amelia backed us away from the train as it grunted and moved forward.

The boy muttered something and turned up his sleeves; he loaded the boxes onto his trolley, then stacked the suitcases on top. It took him some time, and all the while he kept up a deep-throated monologue about "dumb hicks," like we couldn't hear him. I knew he had it all wrong because my daddy had explained to me about hicks. And I was gonna tell him so, but the look on Amelia's face—tired and a little frightened, like maybe she wasn't sure what we were supposed to do next—gave me pause.

Once all those suitcases and boxes were stacked, we followed silently, staying a few steps behind to pick up anything that might drop. I kept an eye on Amelia's face, hoping she'd start looking more like she knew what to do, but I wasn't encouraged. My little brother—naturally oblivious to my concerns—held what was left of our grease-soaked bag of fried chicken and biscuits Mama had made for us since it was our favorite and Amelia's, too. I carried the cotton blanket we'd curled under the night before, sleeping beneath Amelia's protective arms. Amelia sat straight on the velveteen seats since she wasn't allowed in the berths my daddy purchased for us.

We didn't dare look too closely at what we passed as we walked out of the Trenton Railway Station. Nothing felt friendly. We kept our eyes straight ahead while Amelia pulled our two hands together and pushed us in front of her so she could get her snap coin case out of her big black pocketbook. She didn't say another word until we were outside on the sidewalk and an old Cadillac with solid wings over the back wheels pulled up next to us. The porter must have known the driver who stood beside the car because he nodded toward the trunk for the old man to open it.

"This here is a taxicab. You know where you going?" the boy asked Amelia, sounding irritated, which is the same as being disrespectful.

"Don't look like no taxicab to me," she snapped back at him. I was glad to see her filling out again, reflating.

"Only one there is. Whites got the others. Besides, it'll fit you and them children with all them things."

Amelia stared down at that boy for a moment while she collected her thoughts and then turned her eye on the driver like she was looking at a snake, looking to see if he would strike or just go on about his business. Guess she decided he was more the garden variety, scary to come across but harmless. She dropped our hands again and dug through her bag for the piece of paper my mama gave her.

"Got the address right here," she said, handing it to the driver and grabbing hold of Chuck's wrist.

I wasn't worried. The driver was bent, the way old people get bent, and the skin around his mouth was lined, pulling down his mouth like he'd lost, just plain lost, his joy. But his eyes were kind behind the pearly blue film covering his brown cornea, and I recognized immediately that he would be patient and help us get to wherever we were going.

"Boy, what's that say?" he asked, handing Amelia's scrap of paper to the porter.

"Ethel Davis Road," the porter sounded out.

"Yes'm." The driver nodded toward Amelia. "I knows right where that is. About twenty minutes from here. You got a number? You know which house?"

"Says number two," the boy answered.

"Sure 'nough. That makes sense. One on the corner. House on the corner. A big gray one. It ain't the house that belonged to Ethel Davis, though. No ma'am. That house is further up the same road and been there since before the Revolutionary War, when that whole plot of land, right down to the Delaware River, was a farm. Fact, that whole area out there is called Ethel Davis Gardens, even though there ain't no gardens left and Ethel Davis been dead near on a hundred years. But this here house you want is on the road led up to their doorstep, likely the same road they used for their horses. Lot of houses out there now, though. Lot of houses. Number two is the first one on the corner. And it's got some history, too. Used to be a boarding house during the war. World War Two, that is, not the Great War. Soldiers come up for the weekends from Fort Knox long about 1940 and '41 and kept coming 'til long about VE Day. They'd go walk along the water. Get them some R 'n' R for a day or two. I'd drive them over there, and then back over here. Big house. Yes'm. I knows just where it is. I heard someone bought it. Must be them children's family. That right? Got plenty of rooms. Must be five or six bedrooms. They got more children?"

Amelia took the piece of paper with Mama's writing on it back without answering. She folded it and put it in her bag. "Since you're needing to know all my business, yes, sir, that sounds like the right house. Mr. Bill, these children's daddy and the rest of them were supposed to be here, but since they ain't here yet, you gonna take us? Or you gonna stand here and keep filling our heads up with things you probably don't know nothin' about?"

It wasn't a question. The young porter and the driver nodded to each other like they finally understood who they were talking to, and quickly loaded our belongings in the trunk and on the backseat. Amelia wiped her face with a handkerchief. "You children get on in there. I'm gonna sit up in the front seat. Stretch my legs out. Ain't no way for me to fit back there."

It was a relief to hear Amelia sound more confident. It made me feel like it didn't matter where I was, things would come out feeling normal. So I stuffed the blanket on the seat and didn't care a bit when Chuck climbed in and sat right on it. Besides, Chuck looked so tiny in the middle of that backseat pushed up next to one of our boxes, I couldn't help but want to take care of him a little. His shorts were pulled up and his feet barely reached over the edge of the seat. He was still holding the bag of chicken and, even though I was glad Amelia was acting like her old self, I felt sorry for him, and myself, too. No lake. No swimming. I wanted to go sit out on our old porch swing and look out over the brow of the mountain, listen to the whir of the overhead fan, scrape the tips of my shoes back and forth with the rhythm of the swing and feel the quiet of the August heat. But it was like Amelia said, "Ain't nothing here the same as back there."

I climbed into the car next to Chuck with all my mixed-up feelings and took his hand. I don't remember anything more about the ride from the train station to our new house, except looking at the back of the driver's head while he pointed out one thing or another, and seeing that he had the same black and gray hair shining with sweat on his brown skin that was the same color as Amelia's.

We finally pulled into the small circular driveway at the front of our new house, and it was like waking from one dream going into another. The first thing I heard was the taxi driver telling Amelia she needed to give him an extra fifty cents to help with all the luggage. She said, "No, sir," her voice keeping that no-nonsense tone she'd used at the station. She explained that she'd paid the porter a whole quarter for moving everything in the first place, and he could come back and take it up with my daddy once he got there. The man nodded and said he would, said he understood her position and she wasn't to worry none, which I thought was pretty nice considering she'd been acting so fierce.

Finally, with our belongings by the front door, we looked around the outside of the house—me racing from one side to the other while Amelia hollered for me not to get out of her sight. I found the backyard. It was squared between the garage and a neighbor's hedge with an ancient stone fireplace overgrown with weeds sitting right in the middle of the grass. It wasn't a big yard, and it didn't have a view like where we'd lived in the mountains, but that fireplace looked like it might be a good place for hiding things—an important consideration when living with four siblings, my parents, Amelia, and Peter.

There was more to look at than that yard. Chuck was running up and down the slanted doors that led down to the cellar, trying to look in the windows above them. The doors were locked and the windows were too high, despite standing on tiptoes.

"Git down off there before you fall and break your neck," Amelia shouted, her hands on her hips like she was holding them down.

"I want to go in," Chuck pouted.

"We ain't gonna get in that house 'til your daddy gets here with some keys," Amelia answered, shouting like we were on the other side of the waterfall on the back of the mountain instead of standing right in front of her. I looked at her and was thinking she was crazy, but then I noticed that she really wasn't paying us much attention. She was glancing over her shoulder, like she was expecting something to jump out at her. I grabbed Chuck's hand. Amelia looked more scared than she did at the train station and she was acting like the time she herded us away from an old hive of bees that had got wind of us and started swarming. She never said then what the problem was either, but when she told us what to do she did so in such a way we didn't dare argue.

"Can't I even look in the windows?" Chuck whined. "Mary did. She's tall enough."

"I ain't picking you up. You too big and it's too hot," Amelia answered softly but firmly. "Now come on away from there."

I saw the boys then. I saw them across the street on their bikes. They were older, maybe fifteen or sixteen, wearing undershirts like my daddy's but with the sleeves rolled up on top of their shoulders. And their hair was slicked back like the Brylcreem ads that came on before the movies started.

"May as well sit down and have our lunch," Amelia said while I stared at those boys. "And let's sit ourselves right out the front so we can see when Mr. Bill and your mama come in the driveway." She glanced around again. "I expect them boys are some of our new neighbors. Don't look so friendly, but they better not be messing with me," she said, taking my hand and pulling me along with her out to the driveway and the front of the house.

"What do you mean?"

"Ain't something for you to worry about."

They were gone a moment later. Chuck ran behind a bush that grew up along the side yard. I knew what he was doing. He couldn't wait anymore, and it was easy for him seeing as he was a boy. Amelia didn't say anything. She surveyed our belongings on the brick front steps and then, careful to support herself by leaning hard on one of the overstuffed cardboard boxes, she plopped herself down for a long sit. Her dress was pulled over her thick legs so she could spread them wide and stay cool.

I'd followed her up the steps and forgot about those boys when I looked through the tiny cottage-pane windows on either side of the front door. "I can see in there, Mimi," I whispered. "But nothing looks right. It sure doesn't look like a house. It's got mailboxes on the wall and a big desk, like at a hotel. Maybe this is the wrong place."

Amelia shifted, fanning herself with a ragged piece of cardboard. "Just like what that cab driver said, that's all. Some kind of boarding house. But Lord knows what your daddy was thinking when he bought this place. Your mama ain't gonna like it, not one bit."

"How come?"

"Cause child," she fanned herself again, "it sure 'nough is a big house, but it ain't got nothing fancy about it. Ain't got no white-lady-like feel to it. And you know your mama be looking for things being fine." She stopped fanning and looked at the cardboard in her hand. "She ain't gonna be happy with some flap off some old box making like a fan."

"Then how come we had to move?" I asked, sitting down next to her and taking the cardboard from her to wave in front of us both. "She liked where we were."

"I done told you this a thousand times now," Amelia answered, leaning slightly toward the flow of air I created. "Your daddy had to find hisself a new job, and your mama didn't get no say about it. That's just how it is. Your daddy couldn't be working no more for his own mama when that woman couldn't agree to nothing. Now I know you're too little to understand what all's been going on, but the men working for your daddy had what they call a strike, and, child, it got ugly. Real ugly."

"You never told me that before. What's a strike?" I fanned harder.

"Well, when folks think they ain't being paid enough, they get mad. And that strike been going on a long time. Course, the longer it goes on, the more likely them men will all lose their jobs, so some of them started carrying on, and it got real dangerous, real dangerous."

"Like when they threw that stick of dynamite and Peter nearly jumped out of his skin when it blew that hole in the front yard?" I asked.

"Uh huh. Like that." Amelia took her glasses off and cleaned them on the hem of her dress. "Now, Mary, your mama and daddy did most everything they could to keep everybody happy, but there comes a time when there ain't no more to do. Your grandmother couldn't see eye to eye with your daddy and she the one that got the last say. Wasn't a place for your daddy to work after that."

I brushed the wrinkles in my skirt out flat over my knees and tried to sit up straight the way Mama did whenever Mopsy, that's what we called my grandmother, was mentioned. "So does Mopsy got all those men working for her now?"

"No. She gave the whole company over to your daddy's brother. He always was her favorite. And that man ain't never done nothing in his whole life that I can tell. It don't seem right, but that's what she done."

"And Daddy left?"

"That's why we here. Your daddy done found hisself a job where he be needing to be near New York City and some airports. He be flying all over the world doing something about selling something. Got hisself a job like that now."

I nodded as if I understood, but I didn't. "So how come Mama won't like this house?"

Amelia patted my knee and looked around for Chuck. "Ain't what she's used to. That's all. It ain't what she's been brought up with."

We took the last two apples out of the lunch bag Chuck had carried around all morning and started our waiting, looking up and down the tree-lined street for a wood-paneled station wagon, taking tiny bites to fill the time. There was only a little space between the houses and no open sky. The yards were neatly trimmed, but the driveways were short. I couldn't see any swooping hills or meandering hedges, and I wondered how we would play hide-and-seek or where we'd go horse-back riding.

"Better save that chicken for later," Amelia stated without looking at us. "No telling how long we be sitting here." The afternoon wore on. Amelia didn't move and she wouldn't let us move, either. More children, boys again, but younger with crew cuts and sunburns across their cheeks, rode past on their bikes, around the corner, then back again.

Chuck dozed tucked securely under Amelia's arm and I counted the ants roaming between the cracks of the bricks, all the while feeling the sun beat down on the backs of my arms. We watched a few cars go by, windows rolled down, and a milk truck, but it wasn't a busy road. Amelia hummed. She liked humming; never said the words, just let the music sit in the back of her throat, deep and rich. Chuck burrowed closer into her waist, into the vibration of her wordless songs, oblivious to the heat. And we waited.

The rest of my family made the trip up from Tennessee in our station wagon. My parents, my older sisters, my older brother, a mongrel dog named Grogan, and Amelia's husband, Peter, who was also a drunk. It was a three-day drive from Chattanooga to Trenton, and Daddy had said they would arrive before we did. There was no way to figure out what the delay was, but we weren't worried, just tired.

Late in the afternoon it was still hot, but a whisper of a breeze announced the promise of evening and another group of children on bikes came up to the edge of the driveway. Again, mostly boys, they looked older than me by a year or two. They stared, twisted and turned on their bikes, swarming, and then went away. But they came back a few minutes later, a larger group, and swarmed again, making me want to hide. Slowly, to avoid drawing attention, I inched myself closer to Amelia. When I wrapped my fingers in the seam of her dress pocket, she told me to ignore them. She wasn't feeling friendly, I guess, because the look in her eye would have scared them away if they'd been close enough to see it. It must have been her silence or the tensing of her muscles that woke Chuck.

"Mimi, bikes! Look!"

"I see them, child."

"Can we get one? Please?"

Amelia hugged him closer to her side and the boys left like they were having a race, standing on the pedals and leaning forward over their handlebars.

We waited some more.

It was still light when Amelia let us finish the cold, two-day-old fried chicken. The skin was shriveled and the meat was dry, but we chewed right down to the bone, and then chewed on that, too. Bored.

I had to go pee something fierce, so I went behind the same bush where Chuck went, knowing for sure it would be plain lucky if nobody saw me. I don't think anybody did, but just as I got back to the steps, those boys on bikes were back. Chuck started pestering Amelia to let him go talk to them.

"They can come over here and say 'How do?' like they is civilized," she said. "Ain't no call for them to circle them bikes around like they's vultures. Ain't no call. . . ."

And hallelujah! Just when Chuck was about to get worked up and tearful, the station wagon pulled into the driveway like a chariot from heaven.

"Thank the good Lord," Amelia whispered, hoisting herself up and smoothing down the front of her dress.

Michael, my older brother who was thin and gangly, was first out of the car, followed by my sisters, Norma and Elizabeth. All three were fighting, shouting at each other with pent-up energy from being cooped up in a car for far too long. Elizabeth, the older twin by ten minutes, looked red in the face—she was ready to lash out. She hesitated for a moment, as if surprised or unsure about being out of her seat, scowled at the house, and shoved past me to look in the windows. Norma followed, giving me only a fleeting glance from behind her tired eyes.

Grogan jumped down from the open tailgate and headed straight to the grass, nearly knocking Chuck down with greeting. Chuck regained his balance as Michael tussled his hair.

I looked at Amelia. She'd already pulled her apron out of her big black handbag, put it on, and held the hem out at arm's length so she could carry the empty green Coca-Cola bottles handed to her by my mother. There were probably about twenty bottles, more than I'd ever seen before. Mama said Coca-Cola would rot our teeth. I guess only my daddy had been drinking them.

Mama still sat in the front passenger seat. As I watched her digging around her feet for more bottles, I noticed how she would quickly glance at the house and then down again. It was as if she was trying to find the right way to react, the best way to take in what she was seeing. I felt a familiar flicker of regret that the quiet of the afternoon was over, and an ache in my heart at seeing my mother so uncertain.

Peter rolled out from the back, stiff and bent. He brushed his knees and stretched. His skinny six-foot-six frame was silhouetted like a tired oak against the afternoon light. "Mr. Bill, we here now?" he asked, his voice rasping.

"We're here," Daddy answered. He sounded tired. And Mama? Well, there were jobs to do to settle us in the house and when there was something needed doing she put being tired behind.

Chuck squirmed around Amelia and tried to climb onto Mama's lap, but Mama already looked like she was getting ready for the task of unpacking and turned away absently, running her hand over Chuck's spiky short hair, then tying her own shoulder-length brown curls back with a scarf. She lifted Chuck off her lap and out of the car. Then she got out herself, moved back to where Peter stood, and started pulling suitcases from the roof rack. I'd been watching everybody so carefully I'd missed my chance for any kind of greeting, and knew from the sadness on Mama's face it was best now to stand out of the way. She was covering her disappointment with work, pushing away her dreams and making do with what my father had chosen without her.

Amelia dumped the bottles down on the lawn and stood next to Mama to take the suitcases. "Peter, you take everything in the house," she instructed without daring to take time for even as much as a hello to the man. Then she handed Mama whatever money she had left in her handbag, muttered something about waiting all afternoon, and grabbed ahold of the large thermos stuck behind a scrunched-up pile of blankets. The inside of the thermos rattled.

"It's been a long trip for all of us, Amelia," Mama said, grabbing the thermos. "I hope there is a trash can somewhere."

"Don't you want me to keep that cap? Still good for something."

"No."

The excitement of their arrival evaporated.

Daddy, his thick-rimmed glasses smudged with fingerprints, fiddled with unfamiliar keys to unlock the front door. With growing frustration, he glanced at Norma and Elizabeth who hovered near him, their white-blond hair in stark contrast to his black hair, their blue eyes like frozen water defiantly piercing the dark-coal color of his own. "Move back," he snapped as if their presence was the cause of the lock being jammed.

They stepped back but not far, never having had the same fear of our father that I harbored. Elizabeth squirmed instead. She insisted that she be the first inside, the first to lay claim to the bedrooms, first to stake out her territory and Norma's. I watched as she looked over at Michael who, always wary of being too close to my father's backhand, waited several feet away. As Elizabeth gave Michael her best "don't you dare even try" expression, my stomach churned. Michael didn't see the look on Daddy's face. Michael, who never paid Elizabeth any mind, was crossing his eyes at her. They wrestled a lot, and at that age she was stronger, but he still did whatever he wanted. With Daddy, however, it was different.

Michael's crew-cut hair spiked where a cowlick pushed it forward and his T-shirt hung loosely on his thin arms. It was easy to tell from the red rims around his eyes and his hollow expression that it had probably been a rough trip. I prayed he would stop making faces, but it was too late.

Daddy got the door open and, as the twins ran inside, he turned and stared at Michael. "Come over here and behave."

"Yes, sir." Michael ceased having any expression.

I pulled on Amelia's dress. She looked down at me and then over to where I was looking. "Mr. Bill," she called, acting as if she didn't know he was fixing to do anything. "I got to tell you about that man who drove us here from the train station, that taxi-cab driver. He be coming back by here, and—"

Daddy turned away from Michael. "What is it, Amelia?" he asked irritably.

"That taxi-cab driver. Now, I know you told me not to be spending a whole lot of money, but we didn't have no way of getting here—"

"Of course. That's fine." Daddy walked toward the car like he'd forgotten all about Michael.

I sighed and Michael took advantage of the moment to slip around behind us, heading to the backyard, out of sight. "Bet you can't catch me," he whispered as he passed me.

"Bet I can," I said. We started to run off but stopped in our tracks.

Two women with perfectly bleached-blond hair, wearing neatly ironed sundresses belted at the waist and carrying large casseroles, came in the driveway.

"Who . . . ?" Michael trailed off.

"Shh. Don't say anything. They must be neighbors," I whispered.

The women bowed their heads toward us, silently handed the casseroles to Amelia without looking at her, and turned to talked to Mama, who smiled politely.

Daddy took out his handkerchief and wiped his forehead. He came forward and introduced himself to the two women while Amelia muttered something about them thinking she was some kind of pack mule. Mama gave Amelia a flash of fierceness the women would not have noticed, then took one of the casseroles from Amelia's arms and put it on the hood of the car.

"This is awfully kind of you, but I don't even know whether the refrigerator is working. Or even if there is one."

"All the more reason you'll need some dinner for tonight," one said.

The kids on bikes showed up again, this time shouting their names and asking ours. They still looked a little scary to me, but my brother Michael seemed happy. Grogan yapped and chased his tail in circles, noticed the door to the house was open, and ran inside. Everyone paused in the sudden quiet, looking like they wanted to go in too, but my mother didn't suggest it.

Amelia put the second casserole down on the steps where we'd been sitting all afternoon while she and Peter finished unloading the car into a big pile.

Tired of waiting, and tired of looking at the other children who were all bigger than me, I was about to sneak in the front door when I was distracted by one of the women whispering to my mother.

"I suppose we should have come over this afternoon," she said, "but we just didn't know what to think about that Negro being here. You understand."

My mother didn't nod or reply, which was a polite way of saying a person was getting too close to giving an opinion on something that wasn't their business.

"Why, I don't think we've ever had coloreds in this neighborhood," the same woman continued, "so you can imagine our surprise. But I just love your Southern accents."

Amelia muttered something about her own surprise then pushed past my mother, hollering for me and my brothers to follow her and find some soap. "You ain't used to this kind of filth," she said defiantly. "We best get rid of it quick."

My mama watched her but said nothing. Daddy followed her with a suitcase and Peter took the garbage over to the garage. Those two women still stood there. I couldn't help but wonder if they understood Amelia's statement of "filth," but their expressions had not changed.

"It would be lovely if you could come over for some coffee maybe in a day or two," Mama suggested in her most charming voice. "We'll have things in better order by then and I'd certainly appreciate suggestions for the house."

"Oh, we'll bring everything. You've got so much to do, you don't want to be worrying about baking. Of course, maybe you don't . . ." they said, looking over to Amelia. "We'll bring the other children, too, to meet yours."

Mama nodded.

Amelia scowled as she pulled the front door closed behind us. She knew it wouldn't take long before those women's children were sent over for afternoons of free babysitting. While we unpacked, she muttered loudly that she'd be knocking some sense into the ladies' children. "Ain't gonna let them turn out like their mamas. No, sir. Lord don't want no more of that kind of fool."

Her expression hardened, like soft wood turned to stone.

Workers in the industrial plants of the Northeast were not generally seen by the public, so the numbers of African Americans in these positions went unnoticed. Further, in retail jobs it became standard practice that African Americans would not have contact with customers, but would instead have "back-room" jobs. In these positions, African Americans were an "invisible" work force, and there was no protection for their jobs. Unprotected wages earned by African Americans in the Northeast were generally 60 percent less than those paid to white men for the same jobs. African American women were paid with even less consistency and at the discretion of their employers. In 1959, Amelia was paid approximately $8.00 a week.

Getting Settled with Ghosts

WE'D BEEN IN the house long enough to have heard stories about the "Great Flood of 1955" when the Delaware River, running alongside our front yard, swelled up and raged against the shorelines like a combative drunk, twisting and turning with belligerence. We heard phrases like "massive destruction" and "unprecedented loss of life." While I was too young to imagine the meaning of such things, the damage to our house—suffered from the onslaught of water tearing through the foundation and rising up through floors—was obvious. It was a large house, and in the Victorian manner it had many bedrooms, long hallways, and too few bathrooms. It stood proudly on the corner of Ethel Davis and River Road, towering above the newer 1950s bungalows of our neighbors while harboring the secret that its glory had been washed away. Every room in our house had suffered from the waters of the Great Flood, even rooms that had remained dry. Cracks snaked up walls on the second floor, the bathroom tiles were tilted and the tub wobbled, and Amelia's room, safe on the third floor, had slightly slanted window ledges and uneven floorboards. The worst damage, however, was to the basement.

The basement was dank and had potholes in the concrete floor. The surfaces of the walls, once strong and level, were crumbling and whitewashed with lime. The window above the deep utility sink strategically positioned alongside the washer and dryer was so thoroughly rotted that my mother stuffed it full of rags to help keep out the seeping mud and the spiders when it rained. The basement was a place to be avoided, a place that scared me if I was alone, a place that Mama said wasn't worth spending money to fix.

Perhaps more disturbing than the damage in the basement were the watermarks on the walls of the first floor that seeped through countless layers of paint, persisting as if alive and determined to be noticed. Amelia said old houses had ghosts, and I decided that several of those watermarks could have been the faces of men and women who had lived in the house before us.

It was early September, a month after we'd moved into the house, when Mama told me to crawl under the kitchen table and use some dark Old English oil on a soft toothbrush to clean the nooks and crannies of the table legs. She said she was teaching me how to take care of the wood the way she had been taught by her mother who had been taught by her grandmother. She said wood needed deep drinks of oil and that dust could easily be removed from the intricate inset designs when the right tools were used. Mama didn't need to say that this chore also gave me something to do and got me out from under foot, and after a few minutes she seemed to forget my presence. I was quiet, comfortably sitting and listening, twisting the dust rag in tight knots around the toothbrush to look like an antique doll.

"You gonna wallpaper?" Amelia asked as she slammed the iron back and forth on my father's shirts, the bottom of her skirt swaying over her thick stockings and worn shoes.

"Well, I don't believe we have much choice," my mother answered.

The room felt like a sauna from the mid-morning humidity, the heat from Amelia's iron, and the steam from the boiling water on the stove, disinfecting the jars my mother would soon fill with the tomatoes she was cutting up. The back door was open, as were the windows, but the only breeze was from a floor fan that stirred up any stray dust balls and the tufts of fur that Grogan, our mongrel dog, shed indiscriminately throughout the house. My skin felt dirty and itchy, but it was nice to be in the shadows and unnoticed.

A drop of oil shimmered on my leg and I rubbed it into my skin, darkening the color. A second drop landed on my shorts, and I tried to brush it off. It spread. The wiping cloth was so saturated that it dripped when I pressed it against the wood. Still, I squeezed it, let the excess oil flow onto the floor, and reasoned I'd wipe it up as I dusted further.

"Wallpaper should cover those marks, but I wonder whether the walls will hold it. We'll have to get all that paint scraped or scrubbed off," Mama said.

"Um hum," Amelia muttered as if she, too, were considering the condition of the walls. But I assumed that she, like me, really didn't want the paint scraped off. After all, wouldn't that let the ghosts out? Wouldn't it be better to just cover them up?

Mama did not elaborate further. She rarely conversed while she was working, and she worked a lot, determined as she was that we would settle well. For Mama, "settling well" meant making the right friends and living with some semblance of the grace and manners to which she was accustomed to and insisted upon. All of that took effort, a Herculean effort that didn't allow for distractions like discussions about ghosts.

"This year I'll learn which are the best recipes, and next year I'll use them for Christmas presents," Mama said from the other side of the half wall as if talking to herself. I stopped spreading the oil, waiting for her to say more about who would receive the tomatoes as presents, and wondering if there was protocol or a correct way to give ghosts gifts, bribes to make them friendly. But in the silence that followed there was only the splat of a tomato dropping on the floor.

"You want me to get that up?" Amelia asked.

"No, I've got it," Mama said.

Within moments, Mama's knife clacked against the wood of the chopping board, and I continued spreading the Old English oil along the seams beneath the table. I felt tempted to rub it on the wall to get it off the floor and to see if the resulting stain would look like the marks in the living room. The oil trickled over my fingers and dripped down my arm. I could hear Mama taking the jars out of the hot water and placing them to cool on the side counter. Amelia hung a shirt up on the doorframe and the morning wore on.

In the silence, I remembered a story Mama told about the Indians in Montana at Last Chance Gulch who raided the general store while my great-grandmother hid inside a pickle barrel. I wondered if there had been ghosts in that town, ghosts who had arrows sticking out of them or were swimming in pickle water. I ran my fingers over the latch that held the two sides of the table together and wondered if my great-grandmother had ever crawled beneath it to hide from those ghosts, or whether it had been positioned in a corner where the shadows kept her safe while she'd listened to her own mother's conversations. I didn't know much more about her, my great-grandmother, other than that she'd eventually lived with my mother and had passed on her stories.

"Hey, Mr. Tom," Amelia called out, interrupting my thoughts to greet the Bond Bread man who was suddenly standing at the kitchen door while Grogan barked and jumped up and down with his tail wagging. "Come on in. Don't pay that dog no mind. He won't hurt you."

"Git down, boy. These ain't for you. Git down." Mr. Tom's voice was deep and rich like Paul Robeson's singing "Suwannee River."

I couldn't see Mr. Tom's face, but I saw his gray pants and the bottom of the large, flat tray that was filled with all kinds of bread, donuts, dinner rolls, and pies. Amelia's feet turned in his direction. She loved

Mr. Tom's once-a-week deliveries.

"Does he come in? Doesn't he hand it to you at the door?" my mother asked in a low whisper. My stomach tightened. If Mama didn't like Mr. Tom, Daddy would make him stop coming.

"No, ma'am. I's got to look and then I decide on what we get."

Mr. Tom hesitated. "Alright?" Clearly he'd heard my mother. He held the screen door open and waited, then slowly ventured inside when nothing more was said. "You must be the lady of the house?" he asked carefully, his feet pointed only slightly to the side of the room where my mother was canning. "I've been doing my business with Miss Amelia here and didn't mean no disrespect. Now, if'n it would be more comfortable, I surely can ask Mr. James to come on in. He out in the truck. Mr. James only allows me to knock on the doors where we knows they is a colored person working. I sure didn't mean no disrespect."

"That won't be necessary," my mother answered in a friendly voice. "It's nice to meet you."

Mama's manners were Southern. In Tennessee she'd been raised by so many housekeepers, she barely remembered their names and rarely spoke of them. She used her manners as a refuge for any shyness and let them guide her through her everyday interactions with others.

I continued to cringe, however, as I was now unsure of her real reaction and knew Mr. Tom would not be allowed to return if she mentioned him negatively to Daddy. Mr. Tom's feet turned back toward Amelia. "You want dinner rolls this week? They is on sale for nineteen cents a dozen," he said, sounding subdued, having lost any expectations.

"Alright with you, Miss Kathryn?" Amelia asked, although she had been buying from the man for the weeks we'd been living there.

"Yes, alright. And get an extra loaf of bread. We'll make French toast for breakfast."

"Yes'm," Amelia agreed. "And one box of powdered donuts," she added.

"I never told you to buy donuts." My mother's voice was sharp.

"No, ma'am. They's for me," Amelia answered calmly as her hand reached down into the depths of her apron pocket and pulled out her black snap coin purse. "I pays for them out of my own money."

My mother didn't answer. I could see Amelia's hands digging out the coins she needed, and I sighed. Relieved. I loved those donuts.

I thought the Bond Bread man would leave then, having put the order on the table and rearranged his tray, but instead, after saying thank you, he turned toward my mother. "Flood hit this area pretty bad," he said, his voice again reminding me of Paul Robeson.

"Yes, it must have been terrible," my mother answered. Amelia put her purse back in her pocket and the ironing board squeaked.

"You need some work done? I'm good with my hands, and I don't charge a lot. Just need to work on the weekends, that's all. Can't work while I'm delivering with Mr. James."

Again, it was quiet. I held the oil-blackened toothbrush mid-air so I'd hear Mama's answer clearly.

"How you thinking you gonna wallpaper the living room, Miss Kathryn?" Amelia ventured carefully. "He could help get them walls ready."

"Perhaps," my mother agreed, but again there was silence.

"Well, I best be going," Mr. Tom finally said, and I lowered my toothbrush, wanting him to work in the house, wanting to maybe hear him sing.

Mama then slowly answered, "It's a good idea."

"Yes'm."

"If you don't charge too much, I can get better wallpaper. I'll give you our phone number, and you call me tomorrow."

"Yes'm. I'll do that," Mr. Tom answered happily. "And let me get you an extra box of donuts half-price. Them children always do enjoy them so."

He left before Mama could answer and I heard the clock in the front hallway chime. The morning had passed.

"Gonna need to make some lunch soon," Amelia stated quietly, as if speaking to herself. "Them children be coming in wanting it on the table. I made up some egg salad last night and I'll put it on this fresh bread."

Mama didn't answer, which meant she agreed.

I don't know if we all liked egg salad, but we ate it. We ate what we were given. Amelia stacked two thick-sliced sandwiches on each of five plates, then added three more to a sixth. She made a large pitcher of water with lemon slices and left it all on the table above me, ready and waiting for my siblings and possibly one or two other neighborhood children. The basket by her feet then began to quickly fill with ironed clothes. The dog outside continued barking, as if the smells of egg salad and tomatoes seasoned with garlic and basil were enough to make him hungry.

"That dog gonna be the death of me," Amelia muttered. "Miss Kathryn," she said more loudly, "you think we got people dead in this house?"

I froze.

"What in the world . . ." I could imagine my mother's hand, the sharp knife stilled above the tomato. "What would make you ask something like that?"

"From the flood. You think maybe someone might of done passed on in this here house, might of died in the waters?"

"Something bothering you, Amelia?"

"No ma'am. Not bothering me like things normal will bother a person but, well, seems like I hear somebody up there at night. Somebody pacing around by them stairs, like he wants to be going on down, but can't." She paused as if thinking, and I sucked my breath in, worried about what she would say next. "And I knows I'm not fixin' my imagination on it. I knows, 'cause them children heard it, too."

My heart beat loudly despite holding the air in my lungs.

"Who?"

"Miss Mary and Mr. Chuck. They's heard it. Both of them. And Miss Norma, she said she done heard something and you know she don't say things that ain't true."

I exhaled loudly. I hadn't known about Norma. My brother and I had heard strange noises, but at that moment, I didn't care. We weren't allowed to be up in Amelia's room after dinner, and now she had given away our secret. I didn't know which was worse: Mama knowing about us sneaking upstairs, Mama knowing about the ghosts, or Norma knowing about them, too.

The sound of chopping continued. I twisted the dust rag tight around my fingers, sure that my mother had been prompted to remember that I was under the table, and I waited.

"Well, Amelia, I don't know about upstairs, but I sometimes think we might have a ghost in the basement," Mama finally offered. "Over by the furnace. But honestly, it's just the house being so old and dank. You know I don't believe in them."

I hadn't thought about ghosts in the basement, but with all the spiders and dampness, it was an obvious place for them.

"But still, sometimes I think I can feel a ghost watching me when I do the laundry," Mama continued.

Amelia stopped moving. "You sure, Miss Kathryn?"

"Seems like it. Might not be the same one that you're hearing, but it could be."

"You telling me you think we got two? Lord, a' mercy. I knew it. I knew there be ghosts here prowling around."

Goosebumps covered me.

"It be the devil. Lord, maybe it be the devil down there," Amelia whimpered, trying to swallow her fear.

"I didn't say that, and I don't want you talking foolishness," my mother countered with unexpected sternness. "It just seems to me that with this house being as old as it is, we are going to *feel* like there might be ghosts. Course I don't think we need to worry about them. If they are here, they can't do anything. Anyway, I guess we haven't been here long enough to know."

"I don't want no ghosts living 'longside me," Amelia proclaimed.

"Amelia!" Again my mother's voice was stern, then slightly, gently teasing. "We've probably been living with ghosts for years and they never have done one thing to harm us."

"What? Miss Kathryn, what you talking about?"

"Well," she continued as if telling a bedtime story, "I've been told ghosts can live in the furniture. And that furniture in Mary's room was out in Montana, and who knows what all went on out there. Snakebites, Indians, fevers. Maybe somebody died in that bed."

My bed? The bed used by my great-grandmother with the head-board that reached the ceiling and was carved with a strange demon. Of course! Of course it had ghosts. The mattress sank down where bodies had lain and it was stained, the dark rings like fading blood. Of course. And the seams that Amelia mended with safety pins were how they got out. Of course.

"Oh, Lord, Miss Kathryn. That bed still got that horsehair mattress on it. Why you keep that mattress if'n you think somebody done died on it?"

My bed. I let the toothbrush drop onto my lap but then oddly, calmly, realized the idea of having ghosts in my bed didn't really bother me. I couldn't remember a time when I didn't sleep in that bed, and I'd never seen a ghost.

"It's just a mattress," my mother stated. "And it's hard to find a new mattress that fits. They don't make them that size anymore."

"But I don't want to be living here with no ghosts, and I sure don't want to be making up no beds where people done died."

I didn't want to hear any more of this conversation. It was too confusing. I knew my mother was teasing, and that Amelia's super-stitions were well known. But I did suddenly wonder about all these ghosts—those in the walls, up the stairs, down in the basement, and in my bed—if they all became friends, would that be enough to create a problem? And Amelia seemed very worried. Scared. She knew more about ghosts than my mother. She'd told me she'd seen plenty.

"Amelia, you do more praying than anyone I know. There is not a ghost anywhere in the world that would dare bother you," my mother then consoled, understanding her teasing had been upsetting.

I made the sign of the cross for instant protection while Amelia considered this statement. "Yes'm," she finally answered, slamming the iron down once again. "The Lord does take care of them that prays. Yes'm, I guess you right."

Our Father, who art in heaven . . .

"Now I want you to tell the children not to be bothering you in your room. They know better. And I don't want you to worry about ghosts. No one has ever proved they are real and if in all your years they haven't bothered you, they won't now."

"Yes'm."

Hallowed be Thy name . . .

I could feel Amelia's relief and let it become my own.

"You know, Miss Kathryn, I sure is glad you gonna get rid of them watermarks. Maybe need to scrape them some, let Mr. Tom scrape them, before you put that wallpaper over them."

"And scrub."

"Maybe. Yes'm, maybe. Long as he don't get it too wet and bring up some more."

I rolled the toothbrush into the rag and placed it carefully by the bottle of English oil, crawled out from under the table, and dashed out the back door before my mother or Amelia could say anything. As the screen door slammed behind me, I could hear the voices of the other children coming home for lunch and I was happy to feel the sun, to let my oil-stained arms wave through the humid air and feel my feet on the dry grass. I knew Amelia would have more to say on the subject of ghosts. But she wouldn't say anything more to my mother. The matter was settled. If there were ghosts, Amelia's prayers would keep them from bothering us.

But that night as I tried to fall asleep, I heard pounding on the metal air vents by the front hall closet. Mama's words had made Amelia's ghosts real. I hummed "Suwannee River," then crept out of bed to ask Norma what she thought.

"Ghosts aren't real," she whispered. "They're good for stories and scaring people. Mama likes thinking about them some, but that's just because she gets reminded of what she heard growing up, and that makes her feel a little more at home. Talking about them like that with Mimi just lets her slip back some to when she was younger."

"But you heard them!"

"I never said it was a ghost. I think it was an owl."

Waking with Peter

AMELIA CLAIMED THAT she felt confused most mornings when she opened her eyes. She said there wasn't any pale yellow in the early light and she didn't feel comfortable under the deep slant of the attic ceiling. I recognized her feelings as close to my own. We'd been in New Jersey nearly two months and still the moments between sleeping and waking, moments when familiar details filtered through to give the brain a gentle nudge, felt abrasive, confusing in the absence of familiarity.

My own room, where there were windows adjacent to two corners, one facing south and shadowed by a tree and the other facing east, felt nothing like the room I'd left in Tennessee where the window was next to the head of my bed. The waking nudge of morning light shining on my face had been replaced by the strange half-colors of fading wallpaper.

I didn't know what Amelia's room had been like in Tennessee. She didn't live with us then, but had instead traveled up and down the mountain every day. Her home was in an area of Chattanooga called Missionary Ridge where the landlords were white and the houses were shabby. She'd said she'd moved with us for the same reason she moved to Ohio with another family she'd worked for. "Need to go with the job. Peter don't help none and we can't live without work. I ain't got no more family in Chattanooga, and I wouldn't burden them if I did. Yes'm, I moved with Miss Kathryn to save me some money for that day coming when I can't work no more."

"Don't feel like it's ever gonna be home," Amelia muttered softly one Saturday morning after I shook her shoulder to wake her. Mama had forgotten to tell her she needed her help for a few hours and I'd been sent up to get her. Amelia often said she didn't mind working extra on Saturday as it kept her from thinking. She threw the sheet back and I could see the sweat stains on her long, white cotton nightgown, and then she rose to an upright position.

She kept her voice low, not wanting to disturb Peter who slept beside her. "Lord, I can't even tell what time of day it be. See the way them shadows fall away from the curtains? That ain't nothing like what it does this time of day in Tennessee. And listen to them birds."

I listened. There were birds chirping at the top of the gables and more in the trees. They sounded different, somehow lighter than the birds in Tennessee, but I couldn't be sure.

"Can't tell a one of them. Ain't mockingbirds and ain't morning doves. Sometimes might be a blue jay I hear, but no way for me to know what kind of birds are in these parts."

I nodded, wishing she'd stop talking. Peter was rustling around like he might wake up and I didn't like being around him.

"Only thing I knows is that it's still summer." She stood as she put her glasses on. "Let me get myself moving," she whispered as she turned toward me. "Lord knows, it's gonna be hot today. There weren't even a single slip of a cool breeze last night. Downright useless having nights that ain't cooling, don't you think?"

I nodded again. I was too scared we'd wake up Peter to say anything, and it wasn't like Amelia to complain in the mornings. In the evenings, when her feet hurt and she rubbed them with witch hazel, she might have had something to say about one thing or another, but the mornings she mostly saved for praising the Lord, so it was hard to know how to answer her.

A black floor fan rotated back and forth, buzzing and flapping a sheet of newspaper that was trapped beneath the runner of the rocking chair. "Ain't no point to blowin' along the floor," she muttered, looking at it like you'd look at a dog that's been chewing up your best shoes. "Asked Peter to put it up on one of them boxes. Asked him . . ."

Peter snored, abruptly, loudly, his feet sticking out from under the blue cotton bedspread dotted with raised, white embroidered balls. Amelia pulled the bedspread away from him and I remembered how she'd carefully unpacked it from a cardboard box late our first night in the house when she said she felt so tired she thought she'd lay down and die. "Body needs something of their own to wake to," she'd said. I worried it had failed to give her that comfort.

Peter snored again and when Amelia looked back over her shoulder at him, her face changed. It was clear that when she saw his greasy gray and black hair, and the lines that stayed deep around his eyes even in sleep, it made her feel mad, or sad. I didn't want him to wake up, and tugged at her hand.

"What you want, child?" she whispered.

"Mama says," I answered as quietly as I could, "to tell you she's going to the grocery store and that Norma and Elizabeth are out on their bikes. Michael has to sweep the driveway and Chuck is supposed to put away the baseball bat he left in the yard. Daddy is still asleep."

"Um hum." She patted my arm and looked again at Peter. "Man smells bad."

He did. There was a sharp, sour odor and a rank mustiness in the room that had nothing to do with the scents associated with Amelia. "Yes'm," I agreed.

"Let's move on over there by the railings, get away from him some."

The long cardboard boxes she'd dragged with me and Chuck on the train, like small coffins, were still packed at the end of the bed. Chuck had marked some of them with crayons, and all of them were tattered with torn corners and ripped surfaces, but Amelia had said she didn't dare unpack, not yet.

A few days earlier she'd explained to both me and Chuck why she wasn't unpacking when Chuck asked to use the boxes to build a house. "Ain't sure what all is gonna happen 'til Peter gets hisself a job. Can't be doing nothing around here once the painting is finished, and he ain't good for much. I know your daddy might be trying to find him something, but your daddy don't know many around here yet. Besides which, Peter come home drunk one night too many and it won't matter if he gots him a job or not, Mr. Bill gonna send us back on down that train line." She'd sighed. "And Peter don't do nothing to help around here. Wouldn't leave him with you children even for a minute. That's my job, so it ain't gonna be hard to send us back if'n it comes to it."

Her concerns had left me feeling uneasy, but I dismissed the idea that she would ever leave. Still, the boxes stayed packed. Chuck had begged to know what was in them, and Amelia said in the top box were many large and a few small squares of material that would be used to make a crazy quilt. She liked quilting, sewing the colors in all directions, except that her fingers got too swollen most days and she said she'd have to wait until the heat died down some before she got started on that project.

Amelia also told us that an old clock was wrapped securely in the material; it was given to her by a woman she had worked for in Ohio. That was when she was first married and Peter was working on the Ohio train lines. "He weren't no porter," she'd explained as if she were talking to herself, thinking out loud. "Nice Negro men worked as porters. No, he helped look after them engines and sometime rode back in the caboose, ready to jump down and clear the rails. But that was a long time ago," she said, "nearly thirty years. . . ." She shook her head thinking about it, and after a few silent minutes, she explained further.

"Ain't nobody should be made to get married to nobody, especially some nobody you don't choose. My daddy did that. He gave my hand to Peter in trade for some money. Course, I was the last child left at home, and I expect he was tired of raising me. Thirteen children and I was the last one. Didn't go past second grade and didn't have time to grow up, neither. Had to marry that man when I was only fourteen, and him already past thirty."

Chuck said he thought it would be more fun not to have to go to school.

"Well now, child, it maybe seem that way, but I's telling you it ain't."

In another box there was a big yellow punchbowl she liked using for the gatherings at her church. It was packed carefully between the sheets and blankets she'd saved during the years and, while she said it was just too hot to start "foolin' with them blankets," I thought maybe she was waiting to find a new church before she unpacked it.

Peter's belongings were his alone. Amelia said she had nothing to do with the packing of his large leather suitcase held together with tied rope. "I expect he's got his overalls and that gold watch he got somewhere along the line. Probably brought every last one of his shirts and no telling how long before Mr. Bill or Miss Kathryn tells him to throw them out. They like dust rags. Man don't see the point to keeping them clean or buying a new one every few years. Leastways when he worked on the rails his boss made him wash."

In the last box, the only one she kept separate, carefully covered by a blanket and standing alone in the corner, were Sylvester's belongings. And that was the box I wanted her to unpack. That was the most important one. Even while I stood there waiting for her to get up and all the while scared Peter would wake, I was aware of that box and aware of Sylvester's presence despite the fact that I'd never met him and never would.

Amelia had whispered like praying when she'd told us what was in Sylvester's box—his Sunday shirt and bag of special stones, the slingshot he'd made from a birch branch, and the spelling book his teacher had given him.

"There was pleasure," she'd said, when she described that spelling book, "pure pleasure—even though the words didn't mean nothing to me. Just holding onto that book was like putting a picture of my Sylvester's face right in front of me and it made me thankful." She had even hummed a little to herself as she thought about the spelling book. "He'd been so happy. Proud. His thin little chest puffed up and his eyes like bright stars when he told me how the teacher-lady promised to give him that book. And I was proud. That boy, he'd been practicing his words so much that she had taken a real shine to him. A real shine."

It made me feel proud just listening to her story. Amelia said there were some who said Sylvester was "slow" but she knew he wasn't; she knew he would have been reading before long, and it didn't matter none if he'd learned when he was six or ten or whenever. "And he was a good-looking boy, too," she said. "Didn't look much like me or Peter, neither. He had him a nice, strong nose that must have come down the line, from his grandfather or some such, and a skinny little face. But you could tell when he done got growed he would have been handsome, a handsome man. Um hum. Only his lips were the same like mine, but folks said he couldn't belong to nobody else."

I imagined him a little like Chuck, although he must have been much bigger, and I thought of his lips, large and pink like Amelia's with what looked like a brown pencil line drawn around the edges. I was sure my image was wrong, but it was strong. My stomach turned over when, with the image of his face still in my mind, Amelia had gone on to explain that the teacher had given the unused book to her at Sylvester's funeral, one week after his twelfth birthday. "Leastways he turned twelve," she'd said, staring at the box where his treasures were buried, his image suddenly shattering any calm.

"Should've got the law. Should've got the law to take him then," she'd continued, whispering vehemently as if forgetting she was speaking out loud.

"Take who?" Chuck had asked.

Amelia closed her eyes for a moment, a long moment like she was pulling herself back to the present. "Don't pay me no mind, boy. I's just talking foolishness." And after that she was careful not to bring up the subject again, and I think Chuck might have forgotten all about it. But I didn't.

I thought about it whenever I saw Peter and I was thinking about it that morning waking up Amelia. And when I looked again at Peter lying on the bed, his aged skin molting with tiny black moles where the jawbone curved upward toward his hair-filled ears, I couldn't help thinking about it again and again, and wondering what all he had to do with Sylvester being dead.

Peter's gangly arms and legs were spread wide and took up most of the bed and he smelled bad, really bad—not just drinking sour, but like a man who needs to shower twice a day but only manages to rub a washrag under his arms on occasion. I was glad he was lying on the far side of the bed, glad Amelia had moved us toward the stairs, and I was glad I couldn't see his face, that I wasn't within his reach.

Amelia turned away from him. "Gonna say my prayers while I get dressed," she muttered quietly. It was Saturday and she didn't need to hurry, didn't need to find socks and shoes or re-iron the pleats in school uniforms or check whether Michael had brushed his teeth. But she'd agreed to keep an eye on us, make breakfast, and there was a pile of ironing the size of a small mountain stacked in the laundry basket.

"Let me get myself cleaned up and down those stairs," she said as a way of telling me to leave.

I was glad we would both be downstairs before Peter woke up.

Emmett Till was a fourteen-year-old African American boy who was murdered in August 1955 for speaking to a white woman in Mississippi. Violence had long been used in the South to intimidate African Americans into passivity, but this murder was particularly brutal and all the more threatening. Emmett's mother, Mrs. Bradley, bravely brought it to the attention of the Chicago media and to the eyes of the country. The trial would become the first time in the history of Mississippi that a black man, Emmett Till's uncle, Mose Wright, would accuse a white man in court of murdering an African American. Anger and interest were created nationwide and the plight of the African American in the judicial system was clearly highlighted.

Michael

"CHILD, YOU KEEP chewing on your hair like that and it's gonna grow right up out of your mouth. I knowed someone it happened to. Sure 'nough, girl had so much hair coming out of her mouth it was like a thick beard."

I pushed the wet ends of my wispy braids behind my shoulders but would not let Amelia change the subject. It was safe being in her room, and quiet, but it didn't seem fair to be there. It seemed cowardly, as if I should have stayed downstairs to do something to help Michael. "How come Daddy keeps doing that? How come?"

"Can't answer that, child."

"Michael didn't do anything, and Daddy stood right there behind him all the way through dinner, hitting the top of his head with his knuckles."

Amelia was silent. She pulled the thread along the hem of my school uniform and didn't look up even though I know she knew I was crying. "How come you keep tearing out these hems?" she asked, obviously trying to change the subject, distract me. "Your mama's gonna throw a fit if she has to sew them. She already making them dresses, doing that smocking for you."

I did love the dresses Mama made, but I wasn't distracted. "Daddy hits the top of Michael's head, and then he gets mad because Michael can't eat." Once again, I began to suck the ends of my braids, remembering how glad I'd been that the dog was under the kitchen table and nobody had noticed me feeding him my food.

"Your daddy don't see no connection, I guess," Amelia answered in a soft voice.

"Yeah, but Chuck doesn't always eat everything. And he only takes the belt to Michael." My whole body shook, like being cold. Chuck didn't eat everything and wasn't punished. As a child I didn't understand, as Amelia did, that Michael's eating had nothing to do with the way Daddy treated him.

Every night that my father was home for dinner was a threat to Michael. My father and my mother would have their five o'clock cocktail and if we were lucky they would remain talking to each other in another room while we ate at the kitchen table. If we weren't lucky, they would stand over us correcting our manners while Amelia stayed by the sink washing pots and pans.

My father had little tolerance for the noises and confusion of five children, and seemed to have no tolerance for Michael. If Michael held his fork wrong, my father twisted his knuckles on his scalp. If Michael spoke out of turn, another twist; if he didn't finish all his food, the hairbrush or belt would appear. My mother didn't seem to know how to stop this, and sometimes her interference made it worse. So she gave up trying. She'd stay over by the stove, fixing more food that she and my father would eat later, long after we children rushed to clear the table and close ourselves in our rooms.

Sitting in Amelia's wicker rocking chair with a unopened school book on my lap, I wondered what Michael was doing at that moment and guessed he was probably hiding in the bunk bed where he slept with Chuck. My stomach hurt. I vowed I'd never eat again if Daddy would just stop hitting him.

"There is some fathers who think they is doing right, child. They think they are making them boys grow up. Your daddy thinks he be doing right."

I knew Mimi was telling a lie, trying to soothe.

"Then how come he never hits Chuck? And he never hits anybody else? How come Mama says it's just something about being the oldest boy, that his mother did the same to him?"

Amelia pulled the thread and thought for a moment. "Child, you listen here for a minute. Go on, put your book down and I's gonna tell something. Maybe you too young, maybe you ain't, but you in school now, and you learning, so might be time to be learning more than your spelling and such."

I crossed my legs in front of me and held the edges of the book, all the while hoping Amelia was going to explain everything so that dinnertime wasn't so terrible.

"There weren't no good in your grandmother. Lord, have mercy. There weren't even an ounce of good in that woman and I don't care how much prayin' she did. Now she might've said she loved your daddy—said it while she was tearing him down—but you see, in the end, it don't matter how much she might've loved him or thought she loved him. She lost him."

A tiny twinge of pity seeped into the anger I felt toward my father.

"And she didn't lose just your daddy. No, sir, seems like she lost your daddy's brother, too. Lost him to the drink. And maybe she done lost your aunt, but I can't speak for her. But I do know your daddy got up and left. He moved to another part of the country to get away from that woman."

My heart beat faster as a new thought emerged. "Do you think Michael will run away?"

"I don't know, but here your daddy is picking on your brother Michael the same way he got picked on, and you up here feeling sick and all the rest of you hiding in your rooms. Tells me ain't nothing been learned." She shook her head and continued sewing. "So now I want you to start learning. Take you some lessons from this. You be looking at it like that and you gonna be able to see what's gonna happen, and maybe there come a time when you can use the lesson. Use the lesson to stop the badness. See now, Michael, one way or another, he's gonna get up and do something same as your daddy. He's probably gonna get up and leave. That be the history repeating itself, and then the other part that history is what the rest of you children gonna do. You see what I'm saying, child? It ain't just Michael that's got caught in this history. And it ain't gonna be just his lesson. This gonna change all you children, just like it changed your daddy's brother and your daddy's sister. This here is a lesson you gonna each have to learn so it don't get repeated."

"What? Don't hit while someone is trying to eat?"

"Well, now, it's more than that, don't you think?"

I knew it was much more, even if I was too young to imagine. I nodded.

"See now, you look at it like this. You be sitting at the table and that fuss is going on, and it don't got nothing to do with you. But you watching. And you feeling bad like it could be happening to you. And you feeling bad cause you can't do nothing about it, leastways not while you is so little. But could be someday you can do something. Maybe you don't know what, but someday. It's like them troubles we got down there in Mississippi and suchlike, and here we are up here in New Jersey . . ." She stopped, looked at me carefully, then continued. "It's like that. And I've been hearing about that in church and hearing what it means to all of us. Now you listen, too. There's a Miss Bradley who's been telling what some men did to her son who was named Emmett Till."

I wondered if his father hit him at dinner the same way, but quickly realized Amelia was telling me something bigger.

"That's right . . . Emmett Till. You might be learning about him one day, but what you be learning here is like what his mama said and what the minister over at my church says—that it's all our business, meaning you can't be sitting at that table and not feel bad about what happened. Things that happen is gonna make you want to do something, just like you want to find a way to stop your daddy. So, you got to find ways . . . Lord, have mercy, you got to find ways."

Again she stopped, and I knew she was thinking about things that had nothing to do with my father, but I couldn't think of anything else. I couldn't think of anyone but Michael. She looked at me to see if I understood, and maybe I did, a little.

"It's alright, child. You just remember there is more than one lesson here. First off, you don't ever be treating any of your own children like that, and you don't let nobody else, neither. You gonna break your child if you do. Or he'll run off. Whichever, it won't be no good. But I expect you already knows that lesson. So you got to be learning the other part of what I'm talking about. What I'm trying to tell you is you can't treat one member of a family in a bad way and not have all the others feeling bad, too."

"So maybe I'll run away, too?"

"Could be. Could be that's just what you decide to do. Mostly though I's hoping you won't never forget to learn whatever lesson you can be learning from what's going on around you. That's all I'm trying to say. You got to learn, and once you learn you'll know how to stop a thing so it don't keep happening." She finished stitching the hem of my uniform while I chewed my hair, wishing it really would grow out of my mouth as even that wouldn't be as bad as how I was feeling.

I wouldn't learn the story of Emmett Till until I was much older, long after my father's history left its mark on all his children.

Coal-burning steam locomotives were common during the first half of the twentieth century. A tender car contained the coal that was shoveled by the "fireman" into the steam-producing furnace. As the technology became more sophisticated, it became more difficult to shovel fast enough to produce the required steam.

Peter's Hands

PETER WAS IN the backyard. I could see him from my window, pulling weeds from crevices between the stones of the old fireplace. Mama was digging in the tomato patch she'd discovered alongside of the garage, and Chuck was kicking a ball around the base of the dogwood tree in the center of the yard. I liked looking down on them from where I sat, up in my room and out of sight. I liked to see what they did, not knowing they were being watched.

Mama was kneeling and using a spade to turn the dirt, her body arched over the green, gangly vines that had shriveled in the August sun while the tomatoes had ripened orange, red, and crimson, firm and round. I imagined her whispering quiet prayers to these plants as she took stakes and forced them down through upturned soil to root level. Her prayers, I assumed, would be about taking hold and staying put; they'd be about getting us settled in this new house and community, and I imagined perhaps this was the way she told God how much she loved her children and what she wanted for them.

Chuck kicked his ball, and it smacked hard against the side of the garage a few feet from where she kneeled. My guess is that Chuck thought he'd win every game once he was allowed to play with the kids in the neighborhood. He ran over and picked up the ball and gave Mama a quick hug around the back of her neck. It was so easy for him; he was "that" kind of child. And when he ran back and drop-kicked the ball in the opposite direction, I could see Peter watching him, taking a swig from the flask he kept tucked in the bib of his overalls. I couldn't imagine what Peter was thinking, which made me stare at him long and hard.

Peter was an ugly old man, skinny as a rail with sharp edges. His elbows stuck out and his arms were too long—like a steam shovel, his upper body bent straight forward with his shiny head hanging down. Even from a distance, his head looked dirty, like he'd put Vaseline in his hair to keep the black and gray curls from springing too far out. Mimi said he ought to keep it cut but that he "didn't care nothing" about what she thought.

Chuck once said Peter reminded him of a turtle without a shell. Maybe. His neck was long with the same turtle-like rough, brown, spotty skin. If I squinted, his hands splayed, brown and tendon-swelled, ropey. Chuck also said Peter smelled like a dead turtle. Maybe.

It was his hands that worried me. I watched him pull the weeds, grass, leaves, whatever had accumulated around the base of that fireplace, and then he used his hands to scoop them into a pile. But the pile didn't get bigger and there was a rake, unused, leaning against the fence behind him. It was as if he really just wanted to feel the leaves against his skin and scatter them. He wasn't about to clean up that yard. His was an odd movement with no purpose. Not like Mama digging around the tomato plants and driving in the stakes to help them grow or Chuck holding the ball waist-high to let it fall for a drop kick so he could perfect the move. No, Peter made it his business to look busy without doing anything, and I remember Amelia describing exactly what I was seeing.

"Man look busy his whole life and ain't got nothing to show for it," she'd said. "Couldn't trust him to get nothing done."

I thought she was being harsh at the time, like she was just mad at him or mad at the world the way she seemed to be some days. But he really wasn't doing *anything*.

"Don't know how he stayed working on that railway," I remembered her saying, "lessen the boss man had him the same way of doing nothing for nobody."

Just then Peter wiped his hands on his overalls, looked over at my mama, and took another swig.

I remembered a story Amelia told once. "Lord, child, I remember once coming home after spending a whole week with your mama. This was back when your sisters were tiny babies, fussin' and carrying on like to put the devil in the ground. Course it weren't their fault none. They got borned with sour stomach and ain't nothing can be done 'cept wait on time to fix it. Well, I came on down the mountain that Friday night, and I was tired. Them girls had been screaming for days. Miss Kathryn, she near about was going crazy and got herself out of the house all day. Mr. Bill, well, he sure seemed to have a lot of work at his office once those babies done got home. And I wasn't supposed to be sleeping up there on the mountain. Wasn't supposed to work past four in the afternoon, but . . . well, don't you know once I'd been there a week or so, your mama started asking me to stay. Now, don't get me wrong, I understood. Them girls were her first babies and ain't nobody gonna be able to handle two babies with that there colic. You got a baby with sour stomach, and you got yourself some real trouble. So I stayed. Help her out some. And I'd been rocking them, and walking them and giving them whatever I could get in them to try and calm them, and Peter was down at the house with nothing to do but wait for me to get home and make his supper. Course the man couldn't think about making none hisself. No, sir. I got down there, my feet hurting and my legs like cement, and he been sitting all day, drinking.

"I says, 'Peter, when you gonna get something done? When you gonna help carry the load some?' And he plain looked at me like I was crazy. Crazy. Man got his reasoning turned so far around he figures his age allows him to let everybody else do for him."

Looking at Peter from my window, I thought maybe she was right. I didn't like the way he was standing there. I didn't like the way he looked at my mama and at Chuck. Not like he was gonna hurt them but like he just plain didn't have a connection to them.

Somebody opened the kitchen door, which was directly below my window, and Grogan ran out. He jumped and barked, and Chuck yelled at him to go fetch. Mama turned some and put her hand up to shade her eyes.

"Amelia, can you make us some lemonade?"

"Yes'm," Amelia said from the kitchen door.

It wasn't hard to imagine what Mimi was doing in the kitchen. I could smell the chicken frying in oil and knew she'd be husking corn.

"You want me to cut up any of them tomatoes?"

"No. We'll let them go another few days."

"Yes'm."

Peter had not moved. He stood like a scarecrow or a dark shadow, looming over the yard. His hands now hung motionless at his side, and I could see how disproportionately large they were to the rest of his body—huge, like shovel heads curved inward. His shoulder slumped forward, and the waist of his overalls billowed out, too large around his emaciated body.

"How come Peter is so skinny and you're so fat?" I remembered Chuck asking Mimi one night when we sat up on her bed looking in the tin cans where she kept her snap beads.

"Ain't a nice way of talking," Mimi answered without any anger, just pointing out something Chuck didn't know. "You don't go around saying things about the ways a person looks lessin' you're saying something nice. Now, Peter, he skinny like he always been. And I got me the weight. Peter, though, he eats like the man been starving his whole life. He eats more than anybody I ever seen. And I don't know where it goes. It's like there ain't nothing that can fill him, nothing that can stick to his bones. Got me a friend back in Tennessee who says it's the bad blood, but they be saying that about near about everything. If he got all that bad blood, seems like he wouldn't be growing so old."

I looked again at how Peter's clothes hung on him and then I noticed the size of his hands. *That's where the food goes*, I reasoned. And I then remembered that the patches of skin running along the inside of his thumbs and out to the tips of his forefingers were darker, much darker than the skin on the backs of his hands.

"That's where the coal shovel blistered him," Amelia had explained when I asked. "Them calluses along his palms turned hard like rock, but they didn't change color like that. Them blisters, though, they kept rubbin' raw 'til by the time they healed the skin done turned plain black."

I could see those patches all the way across the yard from my window, and I watched him lean down, pick up a clump of mud, and rub it along those patches like he was cooling them even though they had healed long ago. I could see him flexing his fingers, like they hurt, and rubbing them the way Mama rubs her neck when she has a headache. And I had no idea what Peter was doing, no idea if he was doing anything, but I guessed he was ready to quit.

Mama never took any notice of him standing there or sipping out of his flask. Chuck and Grogan ran around until Amelia called Chuck in to wash for dinner, which is when I went down to join them. Peter was still standing out by the fireplace.

During the Civil War, a network of safe houses or places to hide called the Under-
ground Railroad was created to help bring Southern slaves to safety in Northern
states. Many of these hiding places could be found in small towns along waterways.
Yardley, in Pennsylvania on the banks of the Delaware River and the canal that
runs parallel, was one such town. Slaves were hidden there in homes and in the crates
used on the waterways. Eventually, a small community of African Americans made
Yardley their home and many who live there today have ancestors from that time.

The Bridge

MR. THOMAS, THE cab driver who had dropped us off at the
house that very first day more than a year earlier, told Amelia where
to find the church—the First Baptist Church of Yardley. He was
standing at the front door with my father one Sunday when I came
down for breakfast dressed and ready for Mass, and he was offering
to pick Mimi up in his Cadillac if she didn't want to walk over the
bridge from New Jersey to Pennsylvania. Having heard only the last
few words of their conversation, I failed to notice the sadness in his
down-turned pursed lips and ignored the unusual look of concern in
my father's face. I instead began clamoring with my immediate opinion that we should join Amelia and walk over the bridge.

"Please. We'll be able to see the whole river," I pleaded, as I began
hopping up and down, a contrivance of young children that convinces
by irritating. "I'm gonna tell Chuck," I continued, "I'll tell him right
now!" Knowing Chuck would be relentless if he joined my efforts, I
continued, "Can we go today? Can we walk over the bridge today?" I'd

wanted to walk over the bridge ever since seeing others on its pedestrian path suspended high above the water.

The bridge was only a short distance from our house and crossed the Delaware River directly into Yardley. It was an old truss bridge with thick pilings that rattled and shook with the weight of traffic. The whole structure had been damaged in the Great Flood of 1955, when the deep water flowing beneath had swelled so high some said it looked as if it was reaching up to touch the wind of the hurricanes that hit that year.

We were, therefore, forbidden to ride our bikes across the bridge, as the two remaining single lanes could barely accommodate the huge cars of the late 1950s and early 1960s. This decree was a source of endless frustration as there were other children in the neighborhood who had permission to use the pedestrian walkway. My father said it was too dangerous. He also explained that there were plans for the bridge to be replaced. And it was hearing those words—that one day the bridge would be gone—that made the desire to walk across the rattling planks ever more urgent. I continued to plead as we stood in the front hallway, ignoring Mr. Thomas's obvious discomfort.

Amelia's lack of reaction to the whole idea quickly slowed my bouncing and whining. She looked at my face without expression, as if I hadn't spoken, as if my movements were taking place on a different planet. She looked at me as if she didn't know why she was standing or who she was—as if she didn't know why Chuck had joined us. She held her hands together, twisting the wedding ring embedded in her finger as if she wanted to sever the bone.

"Daddy, is Mimi alright?" I asked.

My father and the cab driver glanced at one another like they'd been caught and were guilty; of what, I didn't know. Neither moved. They remained by the door as if waiting for instructions, and it was then that I noticed my father wasn't really dressed, that his shirt was buttoned unevenly, and that he'd neglected to wear a belt. Perhaps he saw my eyes drifting from him to Mr. Thomas and back. Perhaps he realized that I was comparing and that there was no comparison. Mr. Thomas was more carefully dressed. Perhaps he understood that in his silence he'd allowed himself to relinquish some of his control. I stood still. Chuck sat down on the stairs. The grandfather clock ticked loudly.

"Amelia?" my father finally snapped, quietly but emphatically. It was that tone that brought her to attention, but still only in a vague sort of way.

"Sure 'nough, child," she muttered with an almost catatonic voice as she patted my shoulder. "Sure 'nough. We'll go on across that there bridge, long as it's fine by Miss Kathryn and Mr. Bill."

The air in the tiny foyer by the front door suddenly felt heavy. It was like spring had jumped forward by several weeks, the lilacs and the fading daffodils in the front garden were too old, and their heavy scent had become concentrated in the small space.

I'd wanted Amelia to be excited. I'd wanted her to want to feel the same as I did, that crossing the bridge was an unexpected adventure, a rare treat, a break from the normal, but was disappointed, wondering again what was wrong, why Amelia's energy had wilted so early in the day.

"I'll go ask Kathryn," my father offered. "Maybe you can go after church. Maybe later this afternoon." He was obviously looking for an excuse to get away from Amelia's fading self and the awkward but sympathetic stares of Mr. Thomas.

Mr. Thomas's head shone the same way it had the day he drove us from the train station. He didn't look any older, but he was old, and he held his hat with his large thumbs securing the brim, keeping his gaze on the floor in a practiced stance as he listened to the grandfather clock ticking away the seconds while my father withdrew from earshot. "I ain't never gonna say one word about none of this," he finally whispered. "Ain't nobody need know nothing about none of it. This between you and Mr. Bill."

I looked at Amelia for an explanation. She pushed my hair back from my face. It seemed to take all her concentration to think of the words she wanted to say in response. "No, sir," she finally said so softly I didn't think anyone could hear her but me, "this between me and Peter." She patted my head, straightened her back, and looked directly at Mr. Thomas. "That man done gone too far this time. Always knowed it would happen. Always knowed. I appreciate you not telling nobody, but this here ain't Mr. Bill's doing. Now I ain't saying Mr. Bill done right, but this ain't nobody's doing, 'cepting Peter. Peter done brought it on hisself."

"Alright then," Mr. Thomas muttered, giving himself a moment to think. "Alright." He put his hand on the doorknob. "You want me to drive you on over to Yardley? They is some fine people over there be happy to make your acquaintance."

"No, sir. Not today. Thank you, but not today."

Amelia let her hands fall to her apron and wiped them on her hip. The movement seemed to bring her back to the present, and she inhaled abruptly, as if she'd been crying. "I expect I be walking on over that there bridge with these children, now that the idea done been born, but it ain't a day for riding in your car. Thank you, but no, sir. Ain't a day for meeting nobody, nowhere."

Her eyes didn't look mad or sad, but vacant, like she was waiting to know how to fill them. Her glasses were fogged, and the lenses were dirty, but I could see how far she'd withdrawn, and the emptiness that remained scared me. It scared me that she was changed, that she had maybe lost whatever it was that kept her coming downstairs in the morning or letting us sit on her bed to watch *Sally Starr* or look at the pictures in her Bible.

Mr. Thomas simply nodded. "Yes'm, I can understand that. Yes'm. Ain't a good day." Again, he paused before continuing. I liked the way he was thoughtful and careful of how he put things, but I still had no idea of what had happened. "I'll be telling my Ruthie you be coming some other time," Mr. Thomas finished as he fumbled with his hat, his thumbs now shifting it almost imperceptibly from one hand to the other as he moved out the door, leaving any afterthoughts unspoken.

"I'll be checking on you," he called back over his shoulder when he reached his Cadillac. "Come by next Sunday less'n I hear from you. Mr. Bill got my phone number. He done wrote it down. So if you don't want me to pick you up, you call me on the telephone."

"Uh huh," Amelia answered, barely audible as she raised her apron to wipe her eyes, turned to climb the stairs as if forgetting Chuck and I were standing with her, and leaned on the handrail for support, lifting her feet with effort.

The three adults had gone their separate ways, and I looked at Chuck, who, confused like me, had been silenced by the scene. Chuck finally shrugged his shoulders. "Let's go get Mama to cut some lilacs. We can take them up to her."

"Ok," I agreed, not having a better idea.

Later that afternoon we did walk over the bridge—Amelia, Chuck, and me—like a small exploratory party going into unknown territories. But only Chuck and I were interested. The planks were higher over the water than I'd imagined, and looking down between them gave me a sense of vertigo, a heart-pounding fear of falling. The wind felt strong, making me even more nervous, or perhaps it was the sway created by the traffic, or the vibrations of turning wheels that shook within my ankles and shins. I didn't like it. I didn't like being perched over rushing water with currents so powerful that huge logs were swiftly carried and bounced against the pilings. I didn't like the lack of distance between the pedestrian railing and the cars, or the too-thin banisters by the outer edge. And I didn't like the noise or the narrow walkway or how Chuck held Amelia's hand while I walked in front. It all felt dangerous and lonely, as if my close proximity to Amelia was still so distant there was no one who could catch me or hold on to me if I fell.

"Hurry up," Chuck yelled from behind me. "Hurry up." And I did, eager to get to the other side, all the while knowing the faster I went the more alone I would be, as Amelia couldn't keep up. She said nothing.

When I reached the other side, jumping over the last few planks, the cement sidewalk felt solid, safe, and secure. I ran ahead to get even farther away from the water and turned around, waiting and watching, grateful for the quiet in my legs, the silence of the wind, and the sound of birds chirping. Chuck let go of Amelia's hand and skipped. Amelia remained silent.

The walkway on the Pennsylvania side of the Delaware crossed over a canal and its towpath that ran parallel to the river. At one time, the canal was used to provide energy to the mills, carry barges full of agricultural goods, and bring commerce to the town of Yardley. At one time, along the fast-moving water, there were warehouse bins with musty interiors that hid runaway slaves—safe cars on the Underground Railroad. But I didn't know that then. I didn't know a tiny population of African Americans traveling the Underground Railroad had settled along the canal near where they hid. They left behind their descendants, some of whom were still there, worshipping at the First Baptist Church where the Great Flood of 1955 had left watermarks high on the altar and where Mr. Thomas had offered to drive Amelia.

Instead of realizing these things, at that moment I was counting the dandelions that had sprouted between the cracks of the thick cement blocks and wondering where the smell of bread was coming from, and why the houses on that side of the river were so different, older than the houses in our neighborhood. And then we arrived in the center of Yardley. Chuck ran up the front steps of a corner store and pressed his head against the glass of the display window. "It's all shoes, Mimi. What's in the next one?"

Amelia's curiosity got the better of her, and for a few minutes her spirits were lifted. "Looks like a post office down yonder. Guess I could find someone knows how to write me a letter?"

"What about Mama?"

"No, child. She's already written so many letters for me I'm wearing down her fingers. And I need to write a letter about Peter, need to explain. . . . Well, I'll find me somebody, now I knows about that church."

"Where is it?"

"How you think I know the answer to that?" she asked with her almost normal huffiness. "Still, I knows it be around here somewhere. Course we ain't seeing much, and most of it's closed anyway 'cause it's Sunday."

"Ah, heck," Chuck fussed.

"Well, you got yourself over that bridge, didn't you?"

"Yes'm."

"That's something, then."

We continued walking around the corner and down one street, past small houses built in pre-Revolution days with porch railings and horse hitches close to the road, past a stone cottage with thick mortar between uneven bricks. Then we were on Canal Street by the "colored" homes, where sagging porches were cluttered with mismatched furniture—used and tired with friendliness—and the smell of hot grease wafted through the Sunday afternoon quiet.

The First Baptist Church of Yardley—a small, white one-room building that may have once been an old schoolhouse—was in the center of these homes, backed onto the canal and sitting high on a stone foundation with steep wood steps and a handrail up to its double front doors. Amelia stood still and stared.

"Now let's get on back," she said softly, as if afraid someone would hear her. "Afternoon's wasting."

"But what about the church?" I asked.

"What about it?"

"Aren't we gonna go in and see it?"

"No, we ain't. I done told that Mr. Thomas I ain't in no kind of mood to meet nobody."

"But . . ."

"No buts. We done crossed that bridge, now let's go on back, now, before somebody comes on out and sees us standing here."

I swallowed my argument, glad at least that Amelia was talking. We reversed positions and I followed behind as we again passed the closed shops.

"I smell a bakery. I know I do."

"Sure 'nough smells like there be one here abouts," Amelia agreed, her interest again waning, but keeping her pace steady.

"If you go to church over here you could go to the bakery," Chuck suggested.

"Sure 'nough."

We crossed back over the bridge. I was glad to walk behind as the vibrations of the cars felt less threatening when I could see the wind plastering the back of Amelia's dress to her legs and her bottom swaying back and forth in tune with the rising and falling of her hips. She held a firm grip on Chuck's hand just as she'd done in the train station when we first arrived. I couldn't help but think kindly about Mr. Thomas and wonder again what had happened to keep Amelia from going to church with him.

I asked Michael when we got home. He was out in the driveway throwing a tennis ball against the garage door, and while we both knew Daddy would smack him hard for making marks on the paint, this was clearly a day when rules were being ignored.

"Don't you know anything?" he asked incredulously.

"What?"

"Daddy sent Peter back to Tennessee."

"How come? Is he gonna be gone long?"

"Gone forever. Daddy found him drunk and trying to hit Amelia with a hammer. Then he went with Peter to the train station to 'make sure that man got on the train and good riddance.'" Michael imitated my father's voice. "Then Daddy and the cab driver must have got to talking about Mimi on the way back to the house, and Daddy told him she needed to find a church, that she hadn't been going to one because Peter wouldn't let her and it was high time."

"Oh . . ." I couldn't help but look up at the windows to Amelia's room. "No wonder she's sad."

"I don't know," Michael said, still throwing the ball. "Daddy says she's better off without him." I was too young to know if my father was right or if he had the right to make that decision. I just knew that day I'd seen Amelia empty of any spirit.

It was that night when Amelia first took out her hat. Chuck and I had climbed onto her bed, as we knew Peter wasn't there. She pulled out a round box stored in a corner, then sat with it in the center of her lap in her wicker rocking chair.

"Why don't you look at them pictures in the Bible and tell me what the story is all about?" she suggested to Chuck as she lifted the top from the box.

Chuck repositioned himself and started talking about bread and fish and people turning into pillars of salt. Amelia didn't correct him, didn't seem to hear him. She took out a dark bowler hat with a faded velvet ribbon around the brim. She held it up to eye level and turned it around slowly, checking every inch and dusting it. Chuck moved on to Adam and Eve and the snake while Amelia took three fabric flowers tucked in tissue paper from the bottom of the box, unwrapped them, brushed and tweaked the petals, twisted the wire wrapped in green felt to look like a stem, and positioned each carefully on the front of the hat.

"My Sylvester always did love this hat," she said, interrupting Chuck and holding the hat toward us. "Said it made me look like a movie star."

"It's nice," I answered.

She put it down on her lap. "Go on, child. Keep telling me them stories. I's listening."

"I don't know any more."

"Sure you do. Look at them pictures, and they come to you."

"Here's one out in the hills when the Lord is a shepherd."

"See now," she leaned back in the chair and closed her eyes. Chuck kept talking, mixing up the stories or making them up. He slipped down farther on the bed, clearly beginning to get sleepy. Amelia was quiet. I wanted to ask about Peter or say I was sorry. I wanted to ask what had happened, but I didn't. A tear rolled down the side of her round cheek and she'd stopped rocking. She closed her eyes. She didn't want me to see her. She didn't want anyone to witness whatever it was that she felt about Peter being gone. And then she started humming, humming like she was trying to make a baby sleep, and rocking her chair slightly forward and back, holding her hat and keeping her eyes closed.

Chuck stopped talking and fell asleep. I took the Bible out of his hands and looked at the picture of the green meadows and the holy light of heaven shining above. I looked at the bright colors, the sheep and flowers, and I heard Amelia's low hum of "Swing Low, Sweet Chariot" and the quiet rhythm of the rocking chair.

"Want me to wake him up?" I asked.

"No. Just leave him be." Moving as if in a trance, Amelia put the hat back in the box and pushed herself up and out of her chair. "I's about ready to go on to sleep, too. Don't you think you better get on downstairs? Your mama don't want you staying up so late on a school night."

I looked over at Chuck and didn't mind that she'd said he could stay and not me. "Can we go back, sometime?" I asked, determined not to leave until some comment had been made about the day.

"Yes, child. I expect so. But I's gotta fix up my hat if I'm gonna be crossing that bridge and lettin' that old man, Mr. Thomas, take me to that church over there. Got to make my hat proud so the Lord can find me, 'cause it seems like he may have done lost sight of me this past many months. Seems like . . . well, never you mind what it seems like. I got my hat, and I'll be going on to that First Baptist Church of Yardley."

I slid off the bed and looked back up at her as I started down the steep steps cut into the floor of her room. I knew she would never say anything about what had really happened that day, about how she'd been left alone, with only white children in a white community, and that she'd stood on the outside of the small African American church in Yardley, not ready to go in. "Night, Mimi," I whispered.

I thought she hadn't heard me as I watched her close the lid on the box, still holding it securely on her lap as if letting it go would drain her of the last bit of her strength. And I watched as she again closed her eyes and let her head fall back against the chair.

"G'night, child."

*The first civil rights sit-ins began in February 1960 at Woolworth's in Greens-
boro, North Carolina, when four young African American students sat down at
an all-white lunch counter. This single act challenged longstanding Jim Crow
laws of segregation and inspired similar sit-ins across the South in restaurants,
parks, movie theaters, and other public areas.*

*The year 1960 was also a presidential election year, and African Americans
around the country were inspired by Kennedy's statement in reference to the
growing numbers of sit-ins: "They have shown that the new way for Americans to
stand up for their rights is to sit down." And they appreciated the help he gave to
Reverend Martin Luther King Jr., when King was arrested for participating in a
sit-in in a department store in Atlanta, Georgia.*

Aunt Carrie's House

THE FIRST HOUSE to the right of the First Baptist Church of
Yardley was painted bright blue with red shutters. It had a tiny porch
where three rocking chairs were squeezed into a space large enough
for only one. The front door opened inward to a small living room
with a freestanding fireplace strategically placed to separate the front
area from the kitchen. Windows faced the porch, lined up next to the
front door, but there was little light as the glass was covered by heavy,
worn drapes with faded panels of thick, moss-green damask with
frayed edges. The wood planks on the floor were polished to a shine
and creaked with the weight of Aunt Lottie, who was Mr. Thomas's
mother; Ruthie Thomas; and Amelia. I joined them uninvited, having been dropped off by my father. I couldn't help but notice how
cozy, not small, the house felt.

Still, I never went farther than the living room. I never saw whatever was on the stove in the kitchen spewing waves of delicious sweet
smells that warmed me faster than the fire burning softly behind where
I stood waiting to be told what to do.

"Wasn't that something? Him being all trussed up like a peacock, then Mr. Kennedy telling him he wasn't gonna put up with that foolishness. Wasn't that something?" Aunt Lottie asked, then looked at me over her shoulder. "She alright?"

"Miss Mary? Sure she is," Amelia answered, nodding assurance toward me from the sinking seat of the couch where she sat, her stocking feet up on a crewel-covered footstool, sewing the hem of an unfamiliar dress.

"Alright then," Aunt Lottie continued as she pushed herself up from a rocking chair. She was old, very old, and as she moved slowly toward the kitchen she leaned heavily on a cane that she gripped with hands that looked almost like the translucent feet of a large bird. She was smaller than Amelia and her gray hair was only slightly highlighted with a few stubborn streaks of black. "Ruth's boys and them at the church talking about joining one of them sit-ins. I told them I ain't sure they should get involved in such like, but they got their minds set."

"They do gets themselves to an age and there ain't no telling them what to do," Amelia said.

"I'll tell them what to do if I see fit," Aunt Lottie snapped, looking back at Amelia with fierce eyes.

"Yes'm, and that's your right," Amelia agreed politely, keeping her eyes on her needle.

"They my grandsons and I ain't so old they won't be listening."

I moved aside to let Aunt Lottie pass just as Miss Ruth turned the tap to spill water over a wide, flat sink filled with pots. I could see from where I stood that it was lighter in the kitchen. The windows at the back did not have curtains and, like the church, the house sat on the edge of the canal that ran parallel to the river, so the sun reflected from the muddy water and made the room seem more like a porch. Miss Ruth looked old, but she was big, tall, and what Mama would have called "full figured." I wished I could join her, but Aunt Carrie had not invited me that afternoon and I didn't dare do anything more than what

I was told.

"Well, I can't say I don't want them boys to go. Lord knows it's time all of us joined in this here effort, but I ain't sure they know how to keep low. They ain't like Southern boys. They ain't been pushed down the same way. Don't know nothing about that kind of being kept down 'cept what they been told. Them good boys, but they ain't had it the same way."

"Yes'm. Thank the good Lord."

"Well, never you mind thanking Him just yet. We still got plenty to set right. We'll give thanks when we done made things right. That's what I'm talking about," she snapped as she continued slowly toward the kitchen. "I guess I can't be keeping those boys home if'n I'm wanting the change."

"Yes'm."

I could see Amelia's hat had been carefully placed beneath a chair near the door where her small box suitcase was stored. I wondered where she slept when she came here for Sunday nights.

"Aunt Lottie, you got something I can give this child to do? I knows it's a right imposition having her with me, but it ain't her fault. She a good child." Amelia looked up at me but made no effort to move or get up. I'd never seen her relaxed with friends . . . comfortable.

Aunt Lottie's ancient eyes again glared at me. "Ruthie, give me some of that corn you need huskin'," her rasping voice called to her daughter-in-law in the kitchen. "We'll get her set up out on the porch," she continued as she turned back to Amelia.

Amelia barely glanced in my direction as she nodded.

I couldn't blame Aunt Lottie for being irritated. My father had dropped me off at her front door without any warning and with no explanation other than he didn't want me "underfoot." It was only for the afternoon, only for the few hours Amelia had free before he picked her up again, he'd explained to me, but no one was happy about it. And I was sure he hadn't told Mama what he was doing. He just said he needed some time to read and to think while Mama was out. Then he told Michael to take Chuck out to play and since my sisters were already at a friend's house, he decided to drive me to be with Amelia. It was embarrassing, so the bag of corn and the pot Miss Ruthie handed me were a welcome relief. I retreated quickly to the porch without saying anything to Amelia.

It was October and still warm. Rocking chairs sat low to the floorboards with pillows covering sinking cane seats. Deep, paint-filled lines had been gouged into the armrests—initials, maybe, or stick figures. I ran my fingers along the lines, their sides softened by sanding, and wondered who had put them there, who had dared. I then set myself to the task of husking corn all the while listening to the lapping of the canal water and putting aside the short stalks to skip and float along the water's surface once the leaves were stripped. There was excitement in thinking about the water, excitement that a house sat so close to its shores, and it was easy to enviously imagine how adventure could fill each waking moment. Finally finished, I tucked the pot behind a chair. I had filled it with the fresh ears of corn cleansed of their tassels and silk. I'd put the debris carefully in a paper bag and folded the top down, momentarily wondering if I should take it back inside, then realized that the feeling of being excluded was even worse than the awkwardness of interrupting. I decided to stay outdoors the rest of the afternoon. I pushed the bag on top of the pot, tiptoed down the front steps, and ran swiftly along the stone foundation and clapboard sides of the house to reach the shores of the canal.

The canal water was murky and brown and moved more slowly than I had imagined, and while the broken stalks I threw floated, there was no thrill in watching their travels. I sat down on the moist grass, disappointed, wishing Amelia wanted me to join her.

"Who are you? What are you doin' here?"

The voice startled me. It came from behind.

"Yeah, who are you?"

Another voice. I turned around and saw feet first—two pairs of sneakers with legs that were dark brown and thin—and I looked up to brothers taller than Peter or my father, thin and gangly the way boys are at fifteen or sixteen, twins wearing the same clothes and carrying books at their side.

I stood. "I'm here with Amelia," I answered and stood, taking my place as the youngest.

"Yeah? How come?"

"Just am." Heat rose in my cheeks. "My father brought me."

"Yeah, well, Aunt Lottie is our grandmother and she didn't say nothing about no white girl coming over here today. What are you doing here?"

"Nothing."

"Something. I'm gonna go find out," he started to walk away and the other turned to follow.

"No, don't," I blurted, not wanting to again be the focus of Aunt Lottie's glaring eyes. "Your aunt will get mad. She's already mad. Amelia takes care of me, that's all."

They turned back, the realization of who I was apparent in their glances at each other. "Oh, yeah. We know about you. You got a bunch of brothers and sisters over the other side of the river. Run Miss Amelia off her feet. That's who you are. Yeah, we know about you. How come you don't let her sit down none?"

"What do you mean?"

"We heard about you from our mother. She says Miss Amelia works harder than anybody she knows, and here she got them swollen ankles but can't sit down none."

I had no idea of what they were trying to tell me and shifted from one foot to the other, trying to figure out what taking care of us had to do with her ankles. "Who's your mama?" I asked, trying to compose my thoughts.

"Mrs. Thomas. Miss Ruth Thomas. That's who. And you know

what we are talking about, girl. Aunt Lottie says Miss Amelia sleeps like she so dead tired when she come over here that it plain ain't right. And if you don't know she's tired, you're not payin' attention," said the more talkative brother as he started walking toward the house in disgust, obviously determined to have nothing to do with me. "Doesn't anybody tell you how to act? My mother says Miss Amelia is one of the finest people she ever met. Miss Amelia gives our grandmother money for food and been putting some aside for us, telling us we got to go on and get more schooling, go to college or someplace. She don't hardly know us, and she's already doing that. And you don't let her sit down." He spit to the side and turned away.

I looked down at my own feet. The rest of the afternoon was a blur.

Penicillin was introduced to the general public in the early 1940s. Until then, common illnesses like pneumonia often resulted in death for children, particularly Southern, African American children with limited access to doctors. Childhood mortality rates had dropped significantly by the 1960s as the use of antibiotics became more widespread.

Through the Ice

MAMA SAT CROSS-LEGGED in the middle of my bed surrounded by rolls of wallpaper. She was a few inches away from me and if there hadn't been so much to do, I may have tried to run my finger over her diamond engagement ring or maybe lean toward her to brush against her arm. Instead, I concentrated on navigating my scissors around the intricate edges of the trim for the Victorian-print wallpaper she'd chosen for my room, and found contentment in the sweet aromas of meatloaf and mashed potatoes wafting up from the kitchen.

"I know it's not easy for you to cut that paper, but I can't do it. My fingers are just too big for those scissors," Mama explained. "When you finish, and I glue it up, it will look like draperies all the way around your room." I nodded, smiled as if I could imagine, and continued cutting, all the while looking forward to Amelia's dinner. I was also congratulating myself that I had not joined my brothers and sisters at the pond for ice hockey. After all, moments alone with my mother were rare. She was intensely busy and she was a perfectionist, so many of her projects did

71

not involve children who could easily make mistakes.

Christmas was only ten days away. While the house was beautifully decorated—a tall evergreen laden with dolls from around the world in the living room; a gingerbread house with tiny green icing wreaths on the table in the kitchen; garlands with pears over the fireplace; and bowls of red apples mixed with pinecones in the dining room—the annual eggnog party, our third in New Jersey and already established as a neighborhood holiday event, was scheduled for that weekend. Mama was clearly short on time. Once the border in my bedroom was pasted, however, she would be able to show off the entire house, which after three years of renovations was an accomplishment, and she no doubt looked forward to hearing it praised. "A party gives you a deadline," she'd once explained. And we were working with a very strict deadline.

We cut carefully, the December darkness cushioning our efforts, and talked softly about the importance of making a house presentable, which meant perfect.

"Gordon finds *beau-ti-ful* things, don't you think?" she asked, her Southern accent pulling "beauty" like taffy so that any answer would surely be sweet.

"Yes, ma'am," I obliged honestly as my fingers pressed against the hard steel of the curved fingernail scissors, rubbing the skin on my knuckle into a shiny red sore.

"Everything looks elegant?" Again the favored Southern sweetness.

"Yes, ma'am." And it did. The desk and mailboxes in the front hallway had been removed. The sinks had been pulled out of the walls of the bedrooms and the steps carpeted. Drapes, matching bedspreads, family portraits, silver picture frames, lamp bases from China, candelabras, crewel designs on early American chairs, Audubon prints—all of it made the house "presentable."

"I still wish we had high ceilings," she then lamented. "The most beautiful houses always have high ceilings. High ceilings and Venetian glass chandeliers." Her hands dropped to her lap. "I can remember the ceilings of the house I grew up in. The wall curved to meet it so that it cast shadows that smoothly rounded out corners and edges. The rooms felt so soft with all that air above everything—which sometimes had a kind of smoke haze from the fireplace. You know, the fireplace was so big I could walk into it, and when there were logs burning, being in that room was like standing in a field during winter and knowing you'd always be warm."

I tried to imagine.

"It was a wonderful house. My father built it for my mother. Every window on the backside overlooked the Tennessee River and captured the breezes from the valley. There was so much light . . . we had so much fun."

She looked down at her lap, at the wallpaper and the scissors, and for a moment I hated our house, hated everything about it. It wasn't what she wanted or liked. There were no high ceilings, and only a scant amount of light came in the front windows. There were no sweeping lawns to look across and it was dark with shadows that seemed to accentuate the heavy furniture and make the rooms feel weighted under the "objects de art" that Gordon brought.

"Ah well, Gordon has done a terrific job, don't you think?" she continued.

"Yes, ma'am," I agreed, no longer trusting my judgment.

Gordon was a short man with a large stomach. He had arrived from New York not too many months after we settled in New Jersey, and he very quickly arranged for a crystal chandelier to be hung in the dining room centered over Mama's long mahogany table. He then came and went on a fairly regular basis—delighting in the changes he made all the while running his fingertips along the edge of a table or a cabinet and planning the purchase of some other piece. My mother glowed when he approved of her ideas, ideas for colors or patterns, and while she continued to be wistful about the house of her youth, she managed to create a home where she could at least entertain with some degree of style. Only Amelia showed any dislike for Gordon and relentlessly muttered her unsolicited opinions during his visits.

"Man full of foolishness. That's all. Your mama knows better than he do about what all should go in this here house. Ain't nothing more than a low-down carpetbagger finding hisself a dollar."

Mama maintained that Amelia simply didn't like dusting the furniture Gordon chose for us because it had intricate carvings, and the only way to clean it properly was to use a soft toothbrush. Mama said not to pay any attention to her complaining, but I heard Amelia say something about how Mama was just wasting money, throwing it out the window. Amelia also firmly believed my mother "should trust her own self to choose what all went in the house," and I agreed, but only after I realized Gordon had picked the bordered wallpaper that would turn my room into a kind of Victorian garden and my fingers into blistered agony.

"We'll use your bed for coats," Mama was saying as she continued to maneuver her larger scissors along the top, less-intricate outline of the border. "Ladies should always have a place where they can freshen up, comb their hair, or put on lipstick when they come to a party, and the mirror over your dresser is the best in the house. They can pile their coats on your bed and then use the mirror if they need to." It was vital that we learn every detail in the lessons of being a good hostess, which included thinking through the behavior of guests. Nodding agreement, I tried to ignore the ache where my fingers pressed against scissors.

Winter darkness came early in New Jersey, and the light by my bed was no longer bright enough to clearly see the tiny lines that guided my fingers. Mama was ready to quit for the day, which was fine with me as the smell of Amelia's meatloaf made my stomach rumble. She carefully stacked the completed pieces of border, while I rolled the scraps helter-skelter into a pile. It was in those moments that the kitchen door slammed hard enough to shake the house. Neither of us reacted—a slammed door was common in a house full of children. However, as

I handed Mama the scissors, we heard a running stomp through the downstairs hallway and then up the stairs.

"If Michael still has his boots on, I'll—" Mama started to say, but the sound of Amelia's voice stopped her. Below, in the kitchen, Amelia was yelling as loud as I've ever heard. "Miss Kathryn, help! Help!"

Mama dropped the scissors and paper. Then it was Michael's voice screaming, "Mama, Mama!"

She ran and I ran, too, following her down the stairs and past Michael who cowered in the corner to give us space. "I didn't do it, Mama. I didn't do it," he whimpered.

"What?" Mama asked, still running toward the kitchen. And there was Chuck. Amelia was pulling off his clothes. He was lying on her lap, still, ash blue, his eyes closed.

"Oh Lord, oh Lord." Amelia was frantic, her prayer profound and instinctive.

"What is it?" My mother gasped. I stood frozen, staring from the hallway.

"He's wet. Soaked to the skin. Cold. Freezing cold." Amelia pulled his sweater and shirt over his head, then she laid him on the floor between her feet and pulled off his hand-me-down, too-big-for-him ice skates without untying them. She picked him back up again, moving faster than I'd ever seen her move, and held him to her chest with her skirt pulled up over him as high as she could pull it, rubbing his back up and down. "Oh Lord, Lord . . ."

Mama went straight to the phone to call the doctor. The phone cord didn't stretch far, so she kept leaning and looking, trying to see Chuck but unable to as the gingerbread house in the middle of the table blocked her view.

"Get some blankets. Quick. Get the covers off his bed and your bed. Go on. Quick, girl, move." Amelia's voice startled me into action. Running, I bumped into Michael still lingering in the hallway, still wearing his coat, his eyes huge with fear.

"What happened?"

"He fell in."

"In the pond?" I tried to imagine. "The ice broke?"

"Yeah." Michael turned away from me. "I'll get his covers," he said, his voice flat as he bounded up the stairs with me following. "You get yours."

Mama was kneeling in front of Amelia when we got back to the kitchen. She was briskly rubbing Chuck's arms and legs, and immediately pulled the blanket out of my arms to wrap it around him, cocoon-like. "Turn the lights on by the front door. The doctor is sending an ambulance. Show the men where we are when they get here. Go on, now," she instructed me without taking her eyes off Chuck.

He was so pale. His skin was smooth like wax and his hair stuck straight up, still wet despite the towel rubbing. He looked so scrawny on Amelia's lap. I left the room again, backing away, transfixed by the sight, transfixed by panic that made time move moment by moment.

Michael stayed by the front door looking out for the ambulance. Coat on, shivering, wet. Water had soaked through to his chest where he carried Chuck. His nose was red and running, his lips were chapped and peeling, and his hair was flat where his hat had been.

"Take your coat off," I said and pulled the sleeve over one hand as he unzipped with the other. "How did he fall in? How'd you get him home?"

"We carried him."

"Who?"

"Norma, Lizzy, and me."

"Where are they?" We let the coat drop in the corner and Michael shivered. The ambulance pulled into the driveway with lights flashing before he could answer. Grogan went wild, shocking us both into action with his sudden loud barking and frenzied jumping. Michael grabbed ahold of his collar and dragged him upstairs while I opened the door and pointed toward the kitchen. The men didn't need to be shown and pushed past me, moving fast. I could only follow and watch from behind.

By then, Amelia was completely silent, rocking and rubbing. My mother knelt in front of her, her head on Chuck's chest as if listening to his heart. She stumbled, fell backward onto her bottom as one of the men took Chuck from Amelia's arms and the other quickly put a mask over his face. In the moments it took for my mother to get up Chuck's color got better. He wasn't blue, but he wasn't conscious. A third man came in carrying a small stretcher; I backed against the wall to let him pass. They put Chuck on the stretcher, covered him with their own blankets, and lined up what I later learned was an oxygen tank.

They left, carrying Chuck down the hall and out the front door almost as quickly as they had come in. Mama grabbed her pocketbook and went with them. But Amelia stayed where she was, sitting on the chair, limp.

Michael joined us, still clutching the collar on the dog, and stood in the corner, shivering, his pants darkened with the wetness of having carried his brother.

"Where're the girls?" Amelia finally asked, not looking at him or anyone else.

"They've gone after David," Michael said. "David did it. We were all playing hockey, and . . ."

"Low down white trash," Amelia muttered.

"Lizzy says she's gonna beat—" Michael said with clenched teeth.

"Ain't no use in that. When Mr. Bill gets home . . ." Amelia's voice trailed off and her hands dropped into her lap. "When Mr. Bill gets home . . . nothing. Just nothing. Lord says, 'Do not seek revenge.'" She glanced up. "You go on and get some dry clothes on. Lord will . . . Lord will . . ." She could not continue. "Get you a sweater and . . ."

Michael looked at her, his eyes narrowed. "When Daddy gets home, David will get in trouble. Won't he?"

Amelia didn't answer.

"But . . ."

She shook her head slightly. "Ain't no buts in this, child," she whispered.

"But," Michael's voice cracked. The reality of what Amelia was saying was sinking in. David would not be held accountable. "Chuck will be alright?"

Amelia didn't answer. She didn't look at anyone or anything, but let her hands splay on her lap and her arms dangle uselessly. Michael didn't move, nor did I, and when Amelia finally did say something we weren't really thinking about Daddy anymore, but we weren't not thinking of him either. Such thoughts—thoughts about punishment or vengeance—had quickly become peripheral, as it was Chuck, the image of him on Amelia's lap, that had become the real concern.

"There ain't nothing. . . ." She let her chin drop down to her chest. "They be letting us know. They be letting us know."

Amelia barely moved after that. She completely stopped; stopped making dinner, stopped folding clothes or picking up, stopped looking at us or talking, stopped even praying or muttering. Amelia plain stopped. And after a little while, we stopped, too.

Michael slid down the wall and sat like stone wrapped in one of the blankets we brought for Chuck. My sisters came home, red faced and excited, but when they saw Amelia it was as if they'd run into an invisible wall. They, too, sat down on the floor, one on either side of Michael, pulled off their coats, and didn't say another word. My heart raced and I gently rubbed the blister that had formed on the inside of my thumb, but I didn't dare move.

The meatloaf still sizzled in the oven, but the dough for buttermilk biscuits rose too high and then fell. Only the dog dared to sniff around the kitchen, looking for his food and knocking his bowl with his paw until Norma got up and fed him, turned off the stove, and handed us each a glass of milk. I was tempted to break off a piece of the gingerbread house as I was hungry and it didn't seem fair that the little china family that was so carefully placed inside the baked walls had not learned what had happened to Chuck, that their world was still perfect. Instead I sat still, a solidarity growing in the silence between me, my sisters, and Michael, each of us acutely aware that whatever happened next would have nothing to do with us, yet there could be drastic effects. I made silent promises to make Chuck Christmas presents if he got well.

Finally, Mama called from the hospital. She said Chuck had been put inside an oxygen tent to help him breathe, but that he had pneumonia and his lungs were full. I didn't know what that meant, but Amelia groaned. Still sitting, still held in her paralyzing panic, the noise came from so deep within her body that it sent shudders through me. Michael crept to her, sat by her feet, and then tried to get her moving by pulling on her hand and telling her she should change out of her wet dress, but she stared like she didn't know any of us, and nothing had changed when Daddy arrived home.

Lizzy and Norma told him what had happened. They were careful with their stories, careful so it was clear that Lizzy had made David angry, but there was no reason for him to go after Chuck. Chuck was the littlest, the youngest in the neighborhood. He was trying to play hockey with everyone, and when the puck slid onto the thin ice, David told him to go get it. Then when Chuck's foot went through the ice David thought it was funny and pushed him down. The water wasn't deep, but Chuck ended up sitting in it and fell over when he tried to stand up. David laughed so hard he didn't help him out. By the time David stopped laughing, Chuck was blue. Everyone else was at the other end of the pond, and no one, not even David who was next to him, had realized Chuck's face was in the water. When Lizzy saw, she skated there as fast as she could, screaming for Michael to help, and David ran off. Michael carried Chuck home, twisting his ankles as he ran on his skate blades, while Lizzy and Norma stayed alongside him until they got to the driveway and then Lizzy went after David while Norma went back to the pond and picked up the hockey sticks, gloves, hats, and pucks and brought them all back home.

"Lizzy, you say anything to David's parents?" my father asked.

"They weren't home. He's in big trouble though, isn't he?"

"I don't think he meant for Chuck to get hurt," he answered dismissively. "Now take those milk glasses and put them in the sink."

"But . . ." Michael snapped to attention. "But if I did that, you'd . . ."

Amelia interrupted, her voice low, her chin still down near her chest. "Peter didn't mean nothing neither. Don't matter. It don't matter if you don't mean nothing. But if you kills someone . . ." her voice faltered.

"Amelia, this isn't the same. You know that," my father answered gently, as gentle as I've ever heard him as we each quietly placed our glass in the sink.

"It's the same if'n he dies. It's the same," she continued, tears running down her cheeks.

My father paled. "He won't die."

Amelia shook her head without looking up. "I's going on upstairs." She started to push herself up out of the chair. "I's . . ."

"I'll let you know, Amelia."

"Yes, sir. I expect you will, Mr. Bill. I expect you will." Her voice sounded like a lone echo bouncing within a deep well.

She left the kitchen just as it was—the flour in the mixing bowl, the potatoes uncooked, and the meatloaf growing cold. She left me and Michael. She left Lizzy and Norma, and she didn't look back. She didn't fix her apron straight on her waist or wipe her hands. We stood and watched her. I couldn't imagine what she was talking about, but understood it was beyond my father's usual harshness or lack of concern. He was clearly shaken, and it was hard to tell whether it was by Amelia or Chuck, but as he covered the food, I knew there was a lot I didn't understand.

"She's thinking about Sylvester," Norma whispered.

"What about him?" Michael asked.

"How he died," Norma answered.

The room seemed to tilt. I'd never thought about how Sylvester died. I'd never asked. Now I wondered if he'd drowned.

"That's not your business," Daddy snapped. Then he mixed himself a martini, just as he did every night, as if nothing had happened. "Get yourselves some cold cereal then go wait in your rooms until your mother gets home."

"Yes, sir," we all muttered in unison.

For nearly a week, no one dared to speak louder than a whisper. Mama stayed at the hospital during the day and came home at night. The eggnog party was canceled and the Christmas season suspended. I filled the empty hours cutting the thick paper vines that would decorate my room. Amelia came downstairs in the mornings then sat on a chair in the living room without moving until dinner when she made some sandwiches. Daddy didn't even get mad at her, and I didn't care that the blisters on my fingers were still raw.

Christmas morning, Amelia was again sitting in the chair. She had not gone to church nor changed her clothes. "Today's my birthday," she whispered when I came into the room.

"But it's Christmas."

"Peoples get born on Christmas, too."

"Happy birthday!" I whispered, eager to look at the presents Santa brought and then sad that we weren't going to have a birthday cake.

"Maybe the Lord will give me a present and let my boy be well."

No one else was awake. I sat next to her, and we stared at the mantle where the night before we'd hung mismatched pairs of socks beneath the perfect garland my mother had made. Mama, who had come home after I'd gone to sleep so that she could shower and change her clothes, had somehow managed to fill the socks with tangerines and boxes of raisins before going back to the hospital, but there were only a few presents under the tree, and the house was quiet.

The phone rang, and I ran to answer it.

"Mary?" Mama was calling from the hospital. Her voice sounded happy. "Merry Christmas!"

"Hi, Mama."

"Let me speak to Amelia."

I handed Amelia the phone and watched as she held the receiver to her ear.

"Praise the Lord," Amelia finally whispered. "Praise the Lord."

A few hours later, Daddy handed out the presents that were under the tree. There was a large box for Amelia and she held it in her lap for many minutes before she opened it.

"Don't know—"

"It came yesterday," my father interrupted.

She pulled the ribbon and carefully wrapped it around her hand before lifting the lid. "Oh, Lord . . . Lordy, Lordy. Who on earth . . . ?"

"There's a card," Lizzy said, grabbing the card from Amelia's lap. "It says, *'Dear Amelia, Merry Christmas. As one Southerner to another, I know how hard it can be to find something that can remind us of home. I hope this spurs fond memories for you. Gordon.'*"

"Gordon? Mister Gordon doing all this here decorating?" she asked.

"Must be," my father answered without further comment.

Amelia carefully pushed aside the tissue paper. "Good heavens above," she exclaimed as she pulled out an antique, oak hat-stand. It looked like a huge thread spool standing upright on a square base, topped with green velvet sewn over a small cushion. At the time, I didn't know what it was, but I was curious about the scratches and chips along the solid base.

"Been used by somebody just like me, somebody likes to take care of they hats, somebody that's got a hat needs taking care of. Mr. Bill, how Mr. Gordon know about my hat?"

"I don't know," my father answered.

"Mama knows you got one," Michael answered.

"Shouldn't be talking about my business . . ." she said, slowly rubbing her fingers over each scratch as if reading its history. "Mr. Bill, you tell that Mr. Gordon that I thanks him. I do thank him."

"You do that yourself, Amelia, next time he comes to the house."

"Sure I can. Sure I can, but might mean more coming from you."

A week later, Chuck came home from the hospital. He spent another two or three weeks in bed, and, while he suffered with asthma and other lung problems for the rest of his childhood, he was lucky to have been treated with penicillin and lucky to have survived. David never got into any trouble, and Amelia never said another word about Gordon decorating the house, nor about Chuck ice-skating. My fingers quickly healed and the wallpaper in my room forever held the memory of the Christmas when the ice broke.

During the early 1960s, tensions between blacks and whites were becoming more widespread and volatile. Martin Luther King, Jr. tried to lead with calm, forgiveness, and a dedication to peace. Malcolm X, once a follower of King, increasingly called for a violent approach to gaining civil rights. White segregationists continued to use both violence and access to an unfair judicial system to block the efforts of both leaders.

The Gardens

A TINY SPACE through the thick hedge that bordered our yard allowed easy access to neighboring yards. Once on the other side, my siblings and I could slip between bushes and tool sheds, jump over border gardens, and skip along grass-worn pathways to quickly reach the center of the neighborhood. It was there that we played games, cemented friendships, and made mischief. Elizabeth was athletic and outspoken and therefore considered a tomboy. She established herself as leader among the children in Ethel Davis Gardens. Only a few older boys could have contested her position, but they were the complacent boys who rode their bikes in a pack, unaware of how disliked they were, so Elizabeth remained in charge for several years.

During the late 1950s and early 1960s there was power in being known as a tomboy. The term created an assumption of strength not normally credited to girls and daring that rivaled mythological persona. The smaller children in the neighborhood loved that it gave Elizabeth enough leadership that she could make decisions for them. Even my father had a hesitating respect for it. Amelia, however, didn't "cotton" to it. "I don't care nothin' about no tomboy foolishness, and that girl should plain watch her temper," she said more than once. Mama agreed with Amelia and routinely washed Elizabeth's mouth out with soap for disagreeable utterances laced with bad language

Elizabeth ignored them both. Her fierce blue eyes flashed with challenge when she didn't get her way and her blond eyebrows arched like broken stalks of hay, creating a look of meanness that she knew was intimidating, one that she practiced unsparingly. Norma, despite being Elizabeth's twin, couldn't stand up to her or perhaps couldn't be bothered; nor would Michael. Norma and Michael were both secure in their place in the neighborhood hierarchy and were equally respected. Elizabeth ruled, however, and while there was a soft side that I imagined she shared with Norma as they lay in their side-by-side beds recounting the events of each day, Elizabeth seemed determined not to show a hint of softness to the other children.

"Got the devil in her," Amelia muttered late one afternoon toward the end of September when my parents were away for a two-week vacation somewhere in Europe. "Girl full of so much sassin' and backtalk she needs a switching same as some low-down dog," she continued as she snapped green beans into a bowl outside the kitchen door and watched Elizabeth whack a baseball toward Michael.

I sat with my legs spread wide playing jacks. I could hear Amelia's mutterings as my small, red rubber ball bounced and my hand dropped for a twosie. I wasn't very good at the game and, having lost control of the ball, I gave up trying to pick up the six-pronged metal pieces when Elizabeth dropped her bat. With hands on her hips, Elizabeth walked over to Amelia, grabbed a bean, and hissed, "What'd you say?"

Amelia barely glanced beyond the rim of the bowl, but her jaw tightened. "Nothing for you to hear," she answered with an equally challenging hiss. "Now go on, and don't be sassin' me lessen' you want me to take a switch to you."

The rest of us watched, always entranced by these encounters. Michael picked up the baseball and tossed it back and forth between his hand and mitt. Norma, who was lying on the slab of stone by the old fireplace, put down the book she'd been reading. Chuck, who always assumed these confrontations were normal entertainment, dropped his mitt and sat down next to Amelia to snap beans.

"I'll 'go on,'" Lizzy huffed, "right now." She flicked a tiny bean stem she'd pulled from between her teeth. "See? I'm going. Norma . . . Michael . . . follow me!" And with dramatic flair she spun around, picked up her bat, and started walking away.

"Just where you think you're going?" Amelia asked.

"To play baseball," she called over her shoulder, dragging the bat to make a line across the grass and heading to the crawl space in the hedge where she would quickly disappear to the other side.

Michael followed, but with hesitation. "We'll be over by the pond," he said, obviously eager to keep up with Elizabeth but not wanting to cross Amelia. "There's gonna be a game."

Chuck stood and grabbed a bean from the bowl. "Can I go too?"

"I ain't heard nothing about no game. Your mama said you children were supposed to stay right here on Sunday afternoon. You got school tomorrow and you got homework to get done," Amelia called to them both as she put down the bowl and started to stand.

"Ah, come on, Mimi, let us go. It's not late and it won't be long," Norma chimed in, having already left her book and run to the opening in the hedge. "Lizzy will slam the rest of them out and then we'll be back."

"Oh, alright. But you children get back here in time for supper. Five-thirty. No later."

"Yes, ma'am," Michael agreed, waiting to push through the hedge until Norma caught up to him.

"I want to go, too!" Chuck yelled.

Michael let Norma go in front of him and looked to Amelia for an answer. "Mimi?"

She nodded.

"Alright. Hurry up," Michael called.

"You look after him," Amelia warned as Chuck ran across the yard.

"Yes, ma'am," Michael agreed.

Amelia went back to snapping beans and humming to herself while I started a new game of jacks. She glanced at me a few times, maybe waiting for me to follow the others, then finally asked, "You ain't going?"

"They won't let me play," I answered.

"Uh huh. Well, they sure ain't gonna let you play if you be sitting here. Now gimme those jacks so nobody step on them and go on and catch up. If nobody put you on they team, well, don't be making a fuss. Go on, now."

And I did. I was glad she told me to, glad to go, and quickly ran to the hole in the hedges. I bent forward and thrust myself through, ignoring the way its tiny dead leaves and dried sticks scratched my back. I ran across the backyard of our nearest neighbors, an elderly couple who rarely said hello. I slipped around the tiny over-manicured garden of the next house, and under the railing of a long fence dividing a single field into two dried, brown yards. These were the homes in Ethel Davis Gardens, a new, post–World War Two development that had been built in the fields behind our house close enough that they were neighbors but along a different road that kept us separate. Ethel Davis Gardens was full of young families. I ran past David and Bob's two-story house where they kept a pet snake and fed it mice; Suzy's rambler that had a pool where we all swam while her mother complained about the mess but was kind enough to let us splash around for nearly three months each year; Mike and Harry's Cape Cod; and Tom, Barbara, and Charlie's split-level. I ran past young dogwood trees strategically planted to one day cast broad canopies, painted mailboxes at the end of blacktopped driveways or cement front walkways. I ran over yards that were prickly with brown stems of grass and bordered by wilted flowers bending over white painted stones. Newer neighborhoods with no shade seemed to suffer the most when there was little rain, and it had been hot and dry for weeks. My lungs hurt and my eyes watered from the glare, but still I ran, hoping to catch up before teams were chosen.

I could hear the voices of the other children before I saw them. They'd crowded together in the field next to a pond that was murky with low levels of water and algae, creating a stench over the field that routinely became the punch line of jokes the boys directed at each other. Elizabeth, as always, stood in the center of the group, dust kicking up at her feet as she shouted that she'd rather have Norma than Suzy. David, a head taller, shouted back that it wasn't a fair pick as Michael wasn't there.

"He'll be here in a minute," Elizabeth shouted with equal force, but with sing-song sarcasm. "I already told you, Michael said he saw smoke and went to see what it was."

By the side of the field, the yellowed leaves of a weeping willow reached down to touch the dry dirt spots made by children scuffing their feet on the ground while sitting on the swing that hung from the lowest limb. I loved that tree, and decided that if I wasn't chosen to be on a team, I'd be happy to sit quietly on the swing. The willow leaves were still pliable enough to weave.

"Yeah, sure he saw smoke. Little liar. And here comes your skinny-brat sister. I bet you want me to pick her, too."

They all turned to me, their stares stopping me in my tracks, forcing the air out of my lungs and making me shiver. I hated David. I hated the way he always found a way to turn the others against me. He was older than everyone else, including Elizabeth and Norma, and he was mean. Blood rushed to my face. David regularly knocked down kids who were half his size, or pushed himself onto seesaws to create imbalance and bone-jarring drops. I wanted to be on Elizabeth's team, even if she never let me bat. She glared at me, probably surprised I was there.

"Mimi made me come," I quickly explained, noting the way the other kids stood back, responding with tribal-like protocol.

"Yeah, well, Amelia's an old bitch," David shouted. "We already got our teams so you go back home and do your playing with that stupid bitch."

I didn't move. Didn't dare turn away. Didn't dare go forward or say a word. I wanted to disappear. I wanted to pretend I'd never come and swear I'd never come again. But I was confused. David hated both of us? Amelia too? I didn't know which was worse, but I knew I couldn't defend either of us—that I wouldn't find any words nor did I have a strong enough voice to be heard.

"My father says there's going to be trouble with Negroes. He works in the city, so he knows. My father says—"

"Shut up," Elizabeth hissed at him. "Shut up." She turned away from him as if daring him to continue. "You," she said only slightly more gently, pointing her glove at me as if she didn't know my name, "get on my side."

I nodded, relieved.

"You know my father's right, don't you?" David continued.

"What the hell do you know?" Elizabeth snapped, whipping herself back around to glare at his face and simultaneously throwing her glove down. I thought she was going to punch him, but she didn't. "Now are we going to play or not?" she snapped instead, chin up and eyes blazing. "Rock, paper, scissors, we bat first. Two out of three."

As they battled it out, the others seemed to forget I was there and my heart stopped pounding. Elizabeth would pitch the first inning and David would be first to bat. I was to stand in right field, Norma in left, and Michael, when he got there, would be on first base. Chuck stood behind Suzy, who was catching, so he could run after the balls she missed.

The crickets had started chirping early while the frogs bellowed low and unhappily. Elizabeth threw the first strike. The sun was sinking in the sky and the ground beneath my feet was hard as rock. It had been weeks since the last rain. I watched the ball. It wasn't likely to be hit in my direction, and my thoughts wandered back to conversations in the kitchen about the trouble being caused by the drought, the trouble with food prices going up, and the trouble being caused by Negroes. I glared at David. Why would his father predict the same trouble my father had predicted? And what did they mean about trouble when it got hot?

"Come on, champ, you can do it," Elizabeth ruthlessly taunted David, forcing my attention back to the game.

"Bitch," David shouted back, the word clearly his current favorite.

"Everybody quiet," Norma yelled. "Quiet!" she yelled again from the left side of the field. "Listen!"

"What?" Elizabeth shouted impatiently.

"Don't you hear him?"

It was Michael. His voice was like an echo, one word being repeated over and over again, spellbindingly clear. "Fire!"

We stood still, mesmerized.

"Fire in the woods!" He ran toward us; his face was red and sweat streamed down the sides. "It's behind the Rileys' house. Hurry! Fire!"

The Riley children glanced from one to the other, then ran to him, past him as the oldest shouted over his shoulder, "Where?"

"Behind your house. I saw it. There's a fire back there!"

"Is anybody there? Where's my mom?" the oldest, Tom, asked without stopping.

"I don't know," Michael called after him.

"Come on," Elizabeth commanded, and we all ran. A dozen children ran down the road toward the woods. "Somebody call the fire department," Suzy shouted, veering off in the direction of her own house. "Mom! Mom!"

"Shit," David yelped loudly, excitedly. "Fire . . . fire," he continued as if barking to no one in particular.

Dark, black, and sooty smoke rose steadily over the treetops. We all followed closely on Michael's sneakered heels, but when we reached the Rileys' yard, Elizabeth turned toward me and Chuck and ordered that we stay behind.

"But—" we objected.

"Stay here. Both of you!" She glared at me. "Keep Chuck with you. I mean it."

I stood where I was told and watched as the other children ran into the woods. None of them hesitated. None of them looked back. It was like a small herd of buffalo stampeding blindly on the hooves of those in front. Chuck moved forward and I grabbed his arm. He pulled away, running. The smoke was thicker and it looked like he was being sucked into a cloud. "Chuck, you're supposed to stay here," I yelled in vain.

"No," he snapped back at me without turning around.

I grabbed him again, but he easily pulled away and I was left jumping up and down screaming for him to come back. Suzy, her short white-blond hair sticking with perspiration to her heat-reddened cheeks, snatched my elbow from behind. "My mom called the fire department. The fire truck is coming. They'll get him out. They're all gonna be in trouble. They're being so stupid. They shouldn't be in there."

Michael then reemerged, running. "It's huge. There are flames everywhere."

"You guys better get out of there," Suzy yelled at him.

"It's okay. We're not near it."

"Where's Chuck?"

"He's standing right there," Michael pointed, and I could just see Chuck's outline in the smoke as a siren whined loudly and the fire truck came around the corner, screeching to a stop. Michael took one look at it and ran back toward the woods. I thought at first he was getting Chuck, but then he ran past him.

"Michael, get Chuck," I yelled as loud as I could. "Chuck, get back here." They both ignored me but Chuck didn't go any farther into the woods.

"They're so stupid," Suzy said as she moved closer to me.

The firefighters came running from behind us. "Get out of the way," a man shouted. "Move over and stand on that driveway. Both of you. Now."

Suzy grabbed my wrist and we backed away, stumbling over each other's feet.

The firefighters pulled hoses and attached them end to end before finally screwing it into the one small hydrant on the curb between houses. "Move, move, move!" one man shouted over and over. They dragged the now very long single hose across the grass and back between the trees.

"There are kids back here! Don't turn on the water yet! Jesus! Get them out of here!"

Another man ran into the woods and a third came toward us. "How many are back there?"

"I don't know," Suzy said.

"Think, girl. Think. Name them."

"Lizzy, Norma, Chuck, David, Bob, Mike, Charlie, Barbara, Tom . . ." Suzy stopped.

"We got a problem," he shouted back to the truck. "Must be a dozen kids in those woods." He started running toward the trees. "Don't move!" he shouted over his shoulder at us. "Turn the hoses on. Watch where you're spraying and get some water on that fire," he shouted.

The hose squirmed and twisted like a giant worm. Water gushed from the nozzle while men lifted and pulled, straightening it as far as possible to reach deep within the woods.

Suzy put her arm over my shoulder. She was a year older and a few inches taller. She didn't say anything as we watched the smoke grow denser, billowing upward, thick as nighttime. My eyes watered. My throat hurt. And I was afraid. Another truck arrived and the men shouted orders to each other.

"Kids are coming out. Make sure they're all out. Hurry up."

I saw Chuck coming toward us and ran out to grab his hand, dragging him back with me as fast as we could move. He didn't object. "You should see it," he shouted. "You should see it." Elizabeth and Norma followed us, as did all the children, herded by the fireman.

"Is that all? Are there any more kids in there?" one of the firefighters asked Suzy.

Suzy looked around, alarmed. Perhaps alarmed that she was asked. Perhaps alarmed that she might not remember. "I don't know," she whimpered. Her mother was coming toward us and Suzy ran to her, crying.

"Everyone is here," Elizabeth said, red in the face and excited. "Everyone is here."

"Yeah," said David.

And we were. We were all standing in a group, some with tears in our eyes from smoke or fear; some without expression as if waiting to be told how to react; and some, like me, mesmerized.

"Alright then, all of you move. Get over there onto the road and get ready to spill the beans. And do it now," the same man said as he motioned for another to go with us.

"Did you see that tree with all the leaves at the top burning?" someone asked in an excited, loud whisper, as if the fire had already become part of neighborhood lore.

"Not another word," the fireman shouted. "Get yourselves in a line and stand still. You're lucky nobody got hurt. Are you crazy? Don't you know how fast a fire can get out of control? You older kids, you got blocks in your heads?"

"Children, apologize," Suzy's mother instructed.

"Oh, they're going to need to do better than that." The man took off his helmet, which had left a deep line across the center of his forehead. Below it, his face had been darkened by soot, like the faces of each of the children surrounding him. Above it, his skin was clean.

"I want to know who started this. Who started this fire?" He glared, his uniform coat looking hot and heavy and his gloved hands on his hips.

No one spoke, and in the silence it was as if a strange collective guilt settled on all of us, as if the mere fact that we were children somehow meant we were guilty.

"I'm telling you, if you don't say who started this fire you are all going to be in a lot of trouble."

Again no one spoke.

"Suzy," her mother said sternly, "tell who started that fire or you won't eat tonight."

"I don't know," Suzy whispered.

"Of course you do. Now start talking."

We looked at our shoes and at the smoke. We looked at each other. Suzy shook her head.

"Alright," the fireman said roughly, "I want the names of all your parents and I want your telephone numbers."

"It was Michael," David interrupted. "He started it. Michael started it."

Michael's face paled. "No, I didn't. That's a lie."

"Then how come you're the only one that saw it? You saw it first," David persisted.

"Yeah, I saw smoke when we were walking over to play baseball, but I didn't start it."

"Sure. Then how come nobody else saw smoke?"

Michael couldn't answer.

"Boy?" The fireman barked, glaring down at Michael.

"I didn't start it. I swear," Michael pleaded.

"Well, we're gonna have to talk some more about it," the fireman continued.

"What do you mean?"

"Well, nobody else is owning up to it, and nobody else is giving any other name. So . . ."

"I didn't do it."

"That's what you say, but we're gonna stand here until the police get here, then we'll let them take you to the station so you can tell the whole story there."

Michael stared at his feet, trying not to cry. "I didn't do it."

Elizabeth inched over and nudged me. "Go get Mimi," she whispered. "Tell her Michael is in trouble. Run as fast as you can." She then moved toward the man and spoke loudly, "Mister, can my sister go home and go to the bathroom? She didn't even go into the woods so we know she didn't do it."

The fireman looked at me and nodded.

"Go."

I ran, ran as fast as I'd ever run, my legs aching and my side burning, and as I ran a fear took hold that was more horrifying than the fire— Michael going to the police station. Michael was in trouble. Daddy would find out. I jumped over a strip of garden and started yelling for Amelia two houses away.

Amelia, who had gone back into the kitchen to make dinner, was at the door by the time I reached it. Her hands were covered with flour, and she was carrying a rolling pin.

"They got Michael. Mimi. Mimi, they got Michael."

"Who got him? Stop yellin' and tell me what you talkin' about."

"Come on, quick. The police are coming and they're gonna take Michael. They got him. David told them he started the fire."

"Oh Lord." Amelia moved. "Where's a fire? Oh Lord." She didn't bother to put down the rolling pin or wipe her hands. She just started walking, fast, like I'd never seen her walk before. She pushed past me and headed out to the road.

"It's shorter this way," I said, pointing toward the hedge.

"They gonna come this way. They be in their car," she explained without pausing. "Oh, Lord." We rushed on. "They got him in the police car? He in their car?"

"I don't know," I answered, slowing my run to be next to her. "The fireman said the police were gonna take him to the station." I could tell she was thinking fast, working to make a plan. "Come on. Come on," I pleaded, wishing she could move faster.

Amelia huffed and puffed. Sweat was streaming down her face before we'd even reached the first corner and we'd barely rounded it when the first police car came toward us.

"I'm gonna stop that car," she muttered to herself. "They got that boy. . . ." She moved to the center of the road and stood with her feet apart, the rolling pin at her side.

"Mimi?"

"You keep off over there on the grass. Don't you come out here and get in my way. You hear me?"

The car came slowly, but it was there before I could answer. Then Amelia's arms were in the air, the rolling pin looking like an odd extension of her hand, and for a moment neither Amelia nor the police car moved. Then the siren blasted—loud, short, and loud again. I jumped. Amelia didn't flinch.

"Get out of the way, you stupid cow," the man driving shouted from his window.

It was the anger in his voice that was shocking, more shocking than the blast of his siren or the ugliness of the words.

"You got my boy?" Amelia asked him, her voice calm but her intentions clear, the rolling pin still poised above her head.

A second officer got out of the car on the passenger side.

"Put that damn thing down and move off the road."

"I'm askin'. You got my boy in the backseat of your car?"

"No, we ain't got your boy. Now move out of the way."

"I ain't moving 'til I know where my boy is."

"I'm telling you for the last time. We don't have a colored boy in our car."

"I ain't talking 'bout no colored boy," she said loudly, lowering the rolling pin and putting her hands on her hips. "I's talking about one of them children I's looking after. I'm talking about a white boy name of Michael."

The officer turned toward the car then back to Amelia. "You looking after him? Boy named Michael?"

"Yes, sir. I am."

"Yeah, well, we got him."

"You give me that boy," Amelia seemed to growl. "You ain't taking him to no police station. His mama and daddy ain't here and I's taking care of him."

"Should have thought of that before you let him play with matches," the officer replied as he drew his baton out from a loop in his belt.

Amelia stared at him. "I don't want no trouble," she said calmly. "That boy didn't start no fire."

The police officer looked over at me. "Looks like he did. This girl with you?"

"Yes, sir."

"That your brother?"

I could see Michael in the backseat. His eyes were huge with fright. I pulled my shoulders together as if the movement could protect me. "Yes, sir."

"Well, don't look so scared. We're not going to hurt him. We're gonna take him to the station and shake him up some. Keep him from doing something dumb like this again. Now tell that woman to move out of the way or we'll take her in too."

His instructions made no sense to me. I wasn't allowed to tell Amelia what to do. "Mimi?" I asked.

But she didn't have time to answer the police officer who was still waiting behind the wheel. He lost patience and pulled the car forward, forcing her to move back. She moved back, but wouldn't move to the side.

I ran over and stood next to her, not in protest, but because I was afraid she would fall. From there, I could see Michael, his eyes watching every movement and his lips quivering. His short crew cut made him look younger than his eleven years and he'd become so thin with growing tall that his cheekbones stood out like the bones of sparrow wings, sharp and small.

"Look, lady," the police officer said as he tapped his baton on the hood of the engine, a signal for the other man to stop. "You're about to find yourself in some real trouble. Now it's hot. It's Sunday and we all want this over with. We're taking this boy down to the station whether you want us to or not. I know his sister there must've told you about the fire," he said, looking at me, "so you know we got to do it. The other kids say he started it."

His thumbs hooked and pushed down on the leather belt pulled tight with loops where it held the baton, and bullets and a gun—all heavy and unnatural on his hips. I noticed he wore a second belt, too, thin and comfortable to hold up his pants. I stared at the gun, distracted by the rush of images of him pointing it or shooting it, which only served to keep me from hearing what he was saying, so I looked away to Mimi who seemed to have solidified.

"This boy started that fire and it could've burned down the whole neighborhood," the officer said. "It's dry as kindling out there. He's in big trouble and it's the kind of trouble that you can't stand here and stop."

I could feel my arms and legs tensing and took hold of Amelia's hand, but before I could tug her, keep her away from that gun, a second patrol car came toward us.

"I don't know nothing about no fire," I heard Amelia lie. "My girl here told me you got him. That's all I knows."

Correcting her would have been easy, but when I looked up at her I saw the fear in her eyes that defied the belligerence of her stance. I kept quiet.

"So, you don't know why we have him."

"No, sir, I don't." She looked down, waited a moment, and changed tactics before going on. "I sure would be appreciating it if you would tell me what all happened," she asked as calmly as I'd ever heard her.

The police officer pulled his notebook from a back pocket and flipped it open, all the while staring at her as if trying to figure out how to proceed. "Fire was reported by a Mrs. Jayne Chair who called at four-fifteen p.m. Trucks arrived about four twenty-eight. Fire was out by four fifty. Fire was in the woods behind the home of Richard Riley. Kid named David says Michael here started the fire." He closed the notebook. "And nobody else is saying differently."

Amelia let her gaze drop to the ground in front of the man's shoes. "Well, sir, I got to respectfully say differently. That boy ain't started no fire." She barely looked up when the police officer in the second squad car got out and joined us. Her defiance was palatable.

Michael still stared straight forward as he sat in the backseat of the first patrol car. I let go of Amelia's hand and inched closer so I could see him better, saw the tearstains that ran down his cheeks and the dirt on his shirt. I slowly walked to the side window and peered in, hoping the police officer wouldn't stop me. Michael's thin legs and knobby knees straddled the middle hump where the drive shaft ran the length of the car, and he chewed on the nails of his right hand. Clearly, he couldn't hear what was being said as the windows were closed, and I suddenly realized how hot he must have been.

"Can Michael open a window?" I whispered without taking my eyes off him. "Is he allowed to open a window?"

"What you saying, girl?" Amelia asked softly, still looking at the ground in front of the police officer. "Got to speak up."

I stood back. "Yes, ma'am," I said looking up at her, trying to remember how my father instructed me in ways to speak loudly, knowing people had a hard time hearing me and not wanting the police officers to get angry. I inhaled deeply and shouted, "Can Michael open a window?"

Amelia let her head drop nearly to her chest while all three police abruptly turned to stare at me. "What the . . ."

"Shhh . . . she's just a kid."

"Damn . . ."

I was suddenly scared I'd done something horrible and ran back over to Amelia, who put her arm over my shoulder. "He looks really hot, Mimi," I whispered. Amelia stayed silent.

"Get the boy out of the car," one of the men ordered.

Michael scrambled out of the backseat, all the while staring up at the man who opened the door. "Can I go?" he asked. "Can I go home?"

"Michael," Amelia interrupted. "You gonna do what these mens tells you to do. Now I done told them you ain't done nothing. You got to be telling them what all you doing in them woods. Go on now, tell them."

Michael looked around at the four men. "I saw smoke. That's all. And I went to see what it was. I don't know how it got started. I didn't do it. I swear on the Bible I didn't do it. My daddy is gonna kill me." He stopped.

Just then the other children, yelling and shouting at each other about every detail of the burning trees and speculating about what was happening to Michael, came around the corner and saw us. They then started running and within moments, they were crowded around, quiet, looking curiously at Michael, and staying back from the police officers.

"What's going on?" Elizabeth finally asked, looking at Amelia.

"Mimi's trying to get Michael," I answered for her.

"Elizabeth," Amelia said sternly without looking at her, as she still stared at the police officer. "Did Michael start that fire?"

"No, ma'am."

"Alright then. Norma, you tell me, did Michael start that fire?"

"No, ma'am."

"Chuck?"

"No, Mimi."

"Miss Suzy?"

"No, I don't think so."

She was silent. The police stared at us.

"I'm getting mad," the police officer stated flatly without emotion. "I'm not out here to debate with a Negro and some kids. I'm taking this boy down to the station. And you're gonna move out of the way, lady, or you're going to the station with him." He turned toward the car and then back again. "Unless, of course, you think you're some kind of Malcolm-X Negro," he sneered.

Amelia's face froze, but she didn't move, didn't utter a sound.

"But he didn't do it," Elizabeth shouted as she threw down her bat and moved to stand next to Michael, her feet apart and hands on her hips.

"Young lady, don't open your mouth again unless I tell you to," the man said, pointing his finger at her.

"But—"

"What'd I say?" he shouted loudly, making all of us jump.

Chuck started crying.

"Ain't no need—" Amelia began.

He whipped his face around toward her, a threatening look in his eyes. "You gonna move or am I gonna take every one of these children with me?"

The rolling pin shook at Amelia's side but still she held onto it. "What I supposed to do?" she pleaded, her voice still steady as she took a step forward. "The boy's in my charge, and I ain't got no way to fetch him."

The air seemed to fill with a collective agony. It felt as if it had begun to swirl in a kind of liquid slow motion, like a whirlpool pulling us all down into a bottomless void where there was no one, no friend or parent, to catch us. I clutched Amelia's skirt where it billowed and it was then that I saw David running, his arms waving, his sneakers smacking against the pavement.

"Wait!" he shouted. "Wait. I got my father. My father's coming. Wait."

No one moved as he caught up to us. "My father's on his way. He'll be here in a minute."

The police officers looked at each other and at Amelia. "And why do we care?"

"He works for the city. He works with the mayor. He said to wait," David answered, breathlessly.

The police officer shrugged his shoulders. "Yeah, well for about sixty seconds."

It was then, in the ensuing silence, that with the grace and speed of a leopard, Elizabeth pulled herself up to her full height and before anyone could stop her, she punched David in the stomach with all her strength.

David doubled over, and no one, not even the police, moved.

Norma, who had squatted next to Chuck, whispered loudly, "Serves him right."

"Shut up," David finally gasped. "Maybe he didn't start it, but he was the first one to see it, and I got my dad, didn't I?" None of the other children said a word, and I worried that the police officers would take Elizabeth, too, but they acted as if they hadn't seen anything.

A moment later, David's father drove up alongside the police car then pulled in front of it next to the curb. Amelia bowed her head. "Thank you, Lord," she whispered as all four officers and David's father walked together far enough away so they could talk without her interference.

I stared at Amelia who still had not left the center of the street and realized what she'd done, realized she'd stopped the police from taking Michael, and realized it was more than my father would have done. And I knew, too, that somehow my father would find a way to blame Michael for everything that had happened. Michael was staring at his feet, looking as if there was nothing left in him, like all the fear of the afternoon had drained his spirit, and then I saw him look up at Amelia and she smiled at him.

"It be all right now," she said softly.

He nodded.

David's father returned and took my brother by the shoulder then moved him away from the patrol car. "Thank you, officers," he said. "Michael, say thank you."

Michael again looked down at the ground. "Thank you," he whispered.

Amelia, too, moved away from the car. "Thank you, sirs. Thank you," she said, drawing attention away from Michael's lack of sincerity.

"Lady, if I ever have to see you again it won't be friendly. You get my meaning?"

"Yes, sir," Amelia answered, her gaze again lowered.

"Now get out of my sight and take that rolling pin and—"

"I'll make sure they all go straight home," David's father interrupted. "Amelia, I'll follow you in my car."

The children of Ethel Davis Gardens peeled away as we walked slowly toward the house. The presence of David's father behind us kept us from saying much or letting our legs release the energy that was charged between us. Michael stayed at Amelia's side. Chuck carried the rolling pin, and my sisters led the way with David between them. When we got to the driveway, David's father parked and got out to talk to Amelia.

"All I can think to say is thank you. Thank you, sir. I'll take these children in now, and there won't be no more trouble. They is lucky to have you. And they be thanking you, too."

"Well, there won't be any more trouble from these children, but Amelia, you know there's gonna be trouble, and soon, so don't be pushing your luck like that again. Those men could have locked you away for the rest of your life for threatening them with a rolling pin. And don't think they wouldn't. They're getting meaner by the day to Negroes and you are not going to be an exception. Don't stir things up like that."

"Yes, sir."

He made no apologies for David, but ran his hand over Michael's head as he moved toward the door. "Get these kids some dinner and make them go to bed early," he said. "Every one of them needs to think about what they did today. It doesn't sound like a single one of them used a bit of good judgment."

"Yes, sir."

Elizabeth closed the door behind him. "David's a stupid idiot, that's all," she said even before turning back toward us. "There wasn't any reason for him to say Michael started it except he is *so* stupid he just had to say something so he could look like some kind of hero or something. In fact, he could have started it himself, the stupid . . ."

Michael looked at her and without saying a word, shrugged his shoulders and went upstairs to his room. Amelia listened to all the retellings of the story, then shook her head. "Ain't one of you acted with a lick of sense."

Later that night, I asked Amelia what the trouble was David had said his father had mentioned and I asked her what the police officer meant about being a Malcolm-X Negro. She looked at me with eyes so tired I wished could have taken back the question. "That there's a mess you don't need to know nothing about," she answered. "Leastways, not tonight."

During the first half of the twentieth century, it was unusual for African American children in the rural Southern states to attend school beyond first or second grade. Most could not, therefore, read or write as adults. This often resulted in signing documents without understanding what had been written. Further, literary tests enforced in Jim Crow states kept these same African Americans from being able to vote.

Blackberries on Block Island

MY TIN POT was dented with small, round craters where I blasted marbles from slingshots, creating sounds like gunshot. The noise was completely the opposite of the *blonk, blink, blonk* of blackberries being carefully dropped into it to form a soft, juicy mound Amelia would later use for cobbler, pancakes, or jam.

Chuck's bucket was large and solid, much bigger than mine. It was a source of pride for him despite the fact that many of the berries he took home in it were those that overflowed the brim of my tin noisemaker. Still, he loved to tell stories and picking berries brought a new source for his tales just a week after we arrived in August of 1960 for our first vacation on Block Island. They would also provide a wonderful, tasty treat for the full month we remained.

During the 1960s, Block Island was still remote, inhabited by only eccentrics and a few families who had discovered its charms while sailing or while reading New England coastal history books. My parents had learned about it from a New York friend and had fallen immedi-

in love with the faded, shingled frame houses crowned with widow's walks and surrounded with ocean views. The bountiful patches of blackberries on the west side of the island were a bonus, furthering my parents' resolve to make the island a home away from home.

At the end of that first week, we marched along with Amelia to the thickest patches of berries, passing stone walls built by farmers who had cleared the land for crops they hoped would take root in harsh, rocky soil. We hummed and sang, swinging and tapping tin pans with our tiny fingernails, imagining the sound of drums.

Our skin, already tanned from long mornings playing on the ancient rock walls and lazy afternoons on the beach, glowed next to the deep purples of the berries. Our lips and tongues changed to the color of their sweetness, and Chuck gathered stories for fantastic retellings. I remember one of his first was when he swore he'd seen a snake beneath the twisted vines. He described the sharp thorns on the plants and the way they tore at his clothes. He showed everyone the tiny scratch on his forearm where he had reached too deeply into the thicket while trying to pluck the one berry Amelia had warned him against, but he didn't repeat Amelia's retelling of her own story.

"Child, you gonna get a snake wrapped tight all the way around you if you keep doing that," she'd fussed as she pulled the vines back and away from his small arms and short legs.

"There aren't any snakes, Mimi," he'd countered as he took her hand.

"Yes, there are," I corrected, feeling superior in my knowledge. "I saw one yesterday. Michael said it was a garter."

"Michael doesn't know," Chuck pouted.

"Knows enough," Amelia had said as she turned and pulled a few berries from the heavily laden vine near her hip. "He's old enough to remember that big old rattler nearly killed you, and he been looking out for them ever since."

"What rattler?" Chuck asked.

Amelia took off her broad-brimmed hat and wiped her brow with a handkerchief she pulled from the pocket of her overalls. Blackberry picking was the only time she ever wore pants, huge denim overalls that she pulled together at the waist with her apron strings. "You know dat story. Heard Michael try to scare you with it."

"Tell us," I pleaded, ignoring the pang of jealousy that always rose in me when I imagined the sharing of secrets or stories in the darkened bedrooms of my brothers and sisters. They shared their rooms. I did not.

"Well, let us sit a spell." She moved toward the stone wall, her huge bottom snug in the heavy material.

"You sit, Mimi. I'll keep picking."

Chuck gave me his bucket and climbed up on the rock next to her. A thicket of berries spread a few feet away, and I was happy to hear Amelia's voice while I pulled and twisted the fruit between my fingers.

"Lord, it's hot today, but not so hot as it was that day when that big ol' rattler slithered right up like the devil—all quiet and evil, downright slimy like the worst kind of no good. I was up on the porch of your mama's house overlooking the side of the mountain. Right up there on the bluff. And it was beautiful up there. I could stand out there all day ironing, looking out over the valley, counting the hours by when the smoke rose on up from the factory down by the river, or plain looking at the clouds. Lord, that was like being in heaven. Didn't make no mind about ironing your daddy's shirts or what have you."

I watched my hands carefully while she talked, avoiding the thorns as I reached through leaves and under. The best berries were shaded. The best berries were hidden from the heat.

"Fact, I was working on one of your daddy's shirts and Lord, if Lizzie didn't start hollering like some sort of wild fool. Last thing you want to be doing around a snake is hollering, but course I didn't know what in Sam Hill she was making such a commotion about. So I run over to see what all was goin' on and there it was, coiled like a rope. Lord, I just about fainted."

In that moment, the darkness beneath the blackberry bushes seemed to come alive. Every blade of underbrush moved. I felt my heart beating and held my hand still, mid-air, listening. Amelia continued the story and I exhaled, knowing my imagination was playing tricks, knowing there were no snakes beneath my feet, but still too afraid to move. I suddenly wondered if the color of my hand was too bright, too much of a contrast to the shadowed underbrush. Then I thought perhaps Amelia's dark-brown skin would be safer, less likely to be spotted by any snake lurking in the shadows of the bushes. But I refused to give into my fear and continued picking.

"There any rattlers on Block Island?" Chuck asked in a subdued voice. I noticed he'd inched closer to her and had lifted his feet up, resting his head on his knees.

"Lord, I hope not. But there your sister was, staring right into them yellow, mean eyes and I told her to shut her mouth quick and hold still, praying she would be still as a fence post. Then I grabbed hold of the hoe Peter left lying against the side of the house. Must be the only time I was glad he was a no-account, lazy fool who left things lying around for me to put away. Well, I grabbed that hoe, and Lord, I didn't want to have anything to do with that snake, but there weren't nothing else to be done."

I imagined her dark-brown hand wrapped around the dried, pale wood of the hoe and the force she would have mustered to swing it. I smiled, twisted a berry from the vine, and looked at my skinny white arms and then at her thick brown arms. "Did you kill it?" I blurted out, just as I pricked my finger on a thorn.

"Clean dead. Then I picked it up and threw it over the side of the mountain, rattler and all."

A tiny red drop of blood formed on my fingertip. "That's the day I burned my hand, isn't it?" I asked, a vague memory flashing through my thoughts.

"Sure 'nough was."

"She burned her hand?" Chuck asked, startled, the fact so far removed from the story as he knew it.

"Um hum. Burned it bad." Amelia brushed the front of her apron and pulled it up to wipe the sweat off her face. She looked at me with watery brown eyes as she cleaned her glasses, and I wondered if her bad eyesight was the real reason she couldn't read. "You went and got hold of that hot iron and without any sense you grabbed it from the wrong side and started shrieking like the devil hisself had wrapped right around you. Palm of your hand blistered like pink balloons. I thought your mama would kill me."

"But you killed the snake," Chuck countered.

"I sure did. And some men come around to look at it to make sure and well, they were real mad I throwed it over the bluff 'cause they were supposed to identify it, let folks know what all kinds of snakes were around them parts, but I wasn't gonna keep it near you children."

The palm of my hand showed no sign of the burn and I tried to remember what it had felt like. "Did Mama get mad about my burn?" I asked, examining the juice stains on my pale pink palms and the darker stains under my nails.

"No, child. Not after she got all the facts straight."

"Didn't you need to sign something saying what kind of snake it was?" I vaguely remembered someone talking about signing papers identifying snakes, although the conversation was probably unrelated.

"Why you ask me that?" she snapped. "You want to hear how I got to put an X on some paper?"

"No, ma'am," I answered, suddenly ashamed of my curiosity.

"Well, I did. I put my X on some piece of paper saying I killed a rattler, only seems like they changed it. Your daddy told me the paper said it was a black snake, like I didn't know the difference. I been around snakes my whole life. Growed up on the land and my own daddy taught me what they look like and what they do. That was a rattler sure as I'm sitting here. I don't care what them men said. And they didn't even see it; didn't bother to climb down the bluff. Just went on and mocked my word 'cause they didn't have no record of some another rattler being around there. Didn't think maybe it could be the first and I knows now it was what they call a timber rattlesnake."

"That's mean," I whispered.

"Ain't just mean, child, it's plain low down to make me look like I's either telling a fib or don't knows what I'm talking about."

"Did Mama get mad at them?" Chuck asked.

"No, she did not. Some feathers ain't worth rustling." Her voice calmed. "And your mama couldn't help but say something about watching you better, but I don't think she was mad none when your sister started telling how that snake was close enough to stretch right up to her throat."

"How old was Lizzy?" Chuck asked.

"Well, let's see. You were just a baby near about two and so you were still supposed to be playing in your crib. Which makes Mary here about four going on five and Lizzy about seven going on eight . . . thereabouts."

"How come she never tells that story?"

"She got scared. That's why," I nearly shouted, not wanting to change the subject, and angry that those men had changed Mimi's story. I shoved my hand into a bush to grab some particularly large berries, belligerently unafraid, and determined I wouldn't share them. Three, four, five, all in my hand. I pulled my hand out of the bush and pushed them into my mouth.

Amelia stood up. "You be careful doing that, child. You check them first for red ants."

There was no need to answer. The berries were fine, firm, and juicy, but I wondered what else Amelia might have signed without knowing what it said. I picked some more and again shoved them in my mouth.

Amelia came over and slapped my hand away from the bushes. "You gonna pick or eat? If'n you're gonna eat, you're gonna be sick before we get out of this sun. Now, that's enough."

Chuck checked each step as he slowly joined us. He was checking for snakes.

"I don't know why Lizzy and Norma can't pick berries, too," I pouted.

"Lord, you want everybody out here fighting over the pots and what have you?" She moved her hands carefully and quickly, gathering a half a dozen berries before dropping them into Chuck's big bucket.

I watched her hands, noting the contrast of her pinkish palms against the dark brown of her wrists and arms. Amelia's wedding ring pushed against layers of swollen skin and I believed she wore it simply because she couldn't get it off, even rubbing it with soap. The thickness of her fingers made the berries look small, and her square, trimmed nails seemed to highlight the tiny seed-filled pockets of each. I wondered if she liked having brown skin and if it felt different in the sun. I wondered if it was true that white cars were cooler than black cars and if the same was true for people. And then I wondered if maybe Amelia had white skin under her clothes.

The idea stayed with me as the sun bore down on our backs and we picked in silence. If Amelia was white under her clothes, then maybe that was why Daddy let her live with us but not Peter, and that's why he didn't say bad things about her except that she didn't wash dishes well and never followed directions. But he said the same about me. And if she was white beneath her clothes, maybe she was more like me, and she could learn to read and write and I could stay up in her room and, with all these possibilities, I wanted it to be real.

I didn't think any more about snakes. Amelia's glasses fogged with heat and she wiped them with her apron, still leaning over the bushes as if standing straight would signal the end of the task. We continued picking, our fingers turning darker with each spurt of juice, until finally Chuck's bucket was full.

"Should we fill yours too?" she asked me.

"No. That's enough."

Later that evening, Chuck told one of his tallest tales. "I saw it under the bush," he said, his eyes lowered while everyone at the table stared at him. "I saw it slithering along but I didn't move and I didn't make a noise."

"You're pretty brave," Lizzy said with admiration.

"I didn't even tell Mimi," he continued, "because I didn't want to scare her."

"Lord, have mercy," Amelia chuckled.

Chuck smiled up at her with such charm that everyone smiled with him, even me, and in that moment I recognized his wishful imagination and my own. Of course, Amelia's skin was the same over her entire body, and when she signed an X it was because she couldn't read or write. I wished she had not learned that others would try to trick her.

While the State of Rhode Island was the first to abolish slavery in 1774 and the first to heed the call by President Lincoln to fight the institution, there is nonetheless a history of slavery and slave trade particularly along the state's coast. Block Island records show that both Native American slaves and African American slaves lived on the island in the eighteenth century. The building of the stone walls that crisscross the island is historically attributed to island farmers clearing their land; however, island lore persists that slaves were responsible for the construction of the stone walls. It is said that the slaves were told that completing a wall would grant their freedom.

Block Island History

WHEN MY FEET slid on the dry soil of the steep cliff ridges, I clutched the branches of small bayberry bushes, refusing to look farther than my toes and the surrounding foliage. The heights of the Mohegan Cliffs were terrifying, but no one else seemed to mind, no one else was scared or breaking out in a sweat. So I ignored my stomach, which had been clenched anyway since the night before, and continued climbing down the narrow pathway.

Listen to the waves. Don't look down. Don't look down. Don't think about last night.

Mama, who, like Lizzy, was fearless, led the way down to the beach. Clearly she had not yet learned about the damage we caused at the Russell farm, and while there was a consensus that we wouldn't be found out, I had my doubts. Mama chattered happily. She explained that the high cliffs were full of island history—bloody stories of Native American massacres and deadly shipwrecks against the rocky shores pounded by rough tides. We listened quietly as she told these stories, the images imposed upon our private concerns, while we kept pace with her as she maneuvered around boulders and ledges that skirted the cliff side.

Hundreds of feet below, the waves slammed into the shore as if daring us to defy them or perhaps hungrily waiting to consume bodies. The sound of the surf surging over the massive rocks and shimmering tide pools drifted up with the rising haze and I imagined falling through the air.

Don't look down.

My arms and my chest felt pulled as if by a magnet.

Don't look down.

Still, I followed, single file and determined. I wore flip-flops and carried my towel. I carefully watched only the feet of my brother Michael who would, no doubt, I thought, be blamed by my father for the damage we all had inflicted.

Michael seemed unconcerned. It was an attitude he'd developed during the past year, as if my father's continual beatings had nothing to do with him, nor affected him. I was too young to believe otherwise, too young to notice the emptiness that had begun to creep into his eyes, and as I watched his wiry legs easily carry him down the path, I wished I could be more like him.

My quick glances out at the wide expanse of the deep blue ocean made me feel brave and I reminded myself that I loved the sound of the waves—the sound of the pounding and the power, the scraping, the sucking. I reminded myself that I loved the salty breeze, the tingle of the sun on my arms, the smell of the heat and the bayberry.

Don't look down. Don't think about last night.

Still, that day, in the aftermath of what felt like our own savage rampage, my overactive imagination allowed the image of Native Americans throwing bodies over the side of the cliff. This image mixed easily with my memories of the setting sun reflecting in the glass of the dark house with so many windows.

Don't look down. Don't think about last night.

Mama's blue Bermuda shorts, a uniform for island days, covered her legs to nearly her knees. She protected her hair from the wind with a scarf tied at the back of her neck and let her white cotton blouse flap open over her one-piece bathing suit. Her tennis shoes were dusted reddish brown from the tiny, smoke-like clouds kicked up from the dry soil. Red clay. The dust settled on the bottom of the picnic basket held at Mama's side and on the edges of the towels drooping over our shoulders.

One after another, nine children followed Mama's lead that day, each carrying towels, drinks, or maybe a ball, but little else as we had been warned we would have to carry back up the cliff whatever we took down. We followed quickly, friends from New Jersey and friends from the island, down between the boulders, zigzagging back and forth along the face of the cliff, all of us eager to reach the beach, all of us eager to be as far away from the telephone as possible.

Suzy and Bob, who were visiting us on Block Island for the first time, were silent as they marched along. Both were from our neighborhood in New Jersey and both Michael's age, which was less than a year younger than Lizzy and Norma, and less than a year older than me. And perhaps that was the problem—this closeness in age, as when we were all mixed up together—it was easy to egg each other on, dare one another and push the limits. I looked at their backs as we all followed my mother and wondered if they would be sent home when our mischief was discovered.

Charlie and Paul, two brothers whose family also spent summers on Block Island, had run ahead, surefooted and nimble. Amelia had warned us all to watch out for Paul as he had a wild streak, a kind of disregard for consequences that wasn't common among the children we knew. And he could be mean, spur-of-the-moment mean, slashing tongue mean, to everyone, even his best friends. He was the same age as Lizzy and Norma, but had declared his real friendship was with Michael. His brother, Charlie, was my age, but he was large—larger than

Paul and larger than Michael. He was as sweet and levelheaded as Paul was crazed, yet he, too, standing next to me, had been seduced into the mayhem of the night before.

We scampered and slid down the pathway to spend a day on the beach below. We pretended we would not get caught, were scared that we would, and were ready to confess, and I wished Amelia could have been with us. I wished Amelia could climb down the cliff and say something to my mother that would put what had happened in perspective before the truth was known.

Don't look down. Don't think about last night.

I kept up, ignoring a stubbed toe and the tiny scratches I got from holding too tightly onto bushes. Finally, we reached the beach. I let the beauty of the place wash over me with a deep sigh, and my whole body relaxed. Chuck, who was behind me, let loose with a loud yell. "Yeah, yippee, let's go!"

Then everyone ran. We jumped over the streams of fresh water that flowed down from the cliffs, kicked off our flip-flops, then raced each other to get to the clearing where the waves landed on smooth sand instead of rocks.

"Put your towels up there," my mother instructed, pointing to a bleached gray log washed up high on the beach. "Keep them out of the wind."

Shorts were kicked off and shirts dropped. Bathing suits readjusted. Lizzy and Norma tucked their towels under the curve of the log. I tucked mine behind a rock.

"If anyone touches my towel, they'll be dead meat," Lizzy warned. The newcomers, Suzy and Bob, didn't know about the blowing sand. They didn't realize that while the granules splayed against our ankles like tiny stinging ants, they would also quickly penetrate the artfully woven sides of the picnic basket and nestle in great clumps between the terrycloth loops of our towels. Only an area out of the wind was good for storage.

Bob spread his towel and placed rocks on the corners.

"You won't be able to dry off if you do that," my mother warned.

"I'll let the sun dry me," Bob said.

"Well, don't say I didn't warn you."

My sisters looked at each other and shrugged. They knew, as I did, that it wouldn't be long before our skin was glazed by the windy salt air, by the sun that looked murky behind the haze, and by the blowing sand. We knew that on this beach, lying down on a towel was not an option. Sitting with a towel wrapped around our shoulders, its edges tucked beneath our bottoms, would provide some welcome relief later in the day, but there would be no sun baking. Bob would learn soon enough.

Suzy copied my sisters and shoved her towel beneath the log, while Paul and Charlie found a large boulder where all the boys, except Bob, stacked their towels, shirts, and flip-flops.

"Come on. Let's go," Paul called loudly over the wind and roar of the surf. "Last one in . . ."

Another small sand cliff ran along the water's edge where the most recent high tide had pushed against the beach. It collapsed with our weight as we bounded toward the waves. The sand between it and the foaming water was smooth, packed down by the pounding surf. I slowly walked forward, waded in the ankle-deep water, and stood silently. All my senses were set ablaze with the power of that ocean—the massive, deep-blue waves rearing up to show a greenish underbody while spewing white crests; the smell of salt and seaweed; the all-encompassing roar; the taste and the feel of the mist that turned the sky pale; and the sensation of the sand ebbing away in swirls over and under my toes. I inhaled these sensations, feeling as if I could draw some strength from them, and inched forward into the water.

My mother, whose mission was to take each of us out into the deep water, under and over the waves until she believed we had mastered the treacherous water, beckoned me to her side. Lizzy, Norma, and Michael had matched Mama's skills during previous visits. They bodysurfed and swam, leaped high with cresting waves, dove beneath those that were crashing, and swam out to calmer waters for rest. I was always terrified, never able to muster the amazing fearlessness they had. Instead, I held my mother's hand as she pulled me over the smaller wake that reached my waist, then pulled me farther, warning me to hold my nose and drop beneath the bending crests, push against the surging walls to come up behind them. Out we went, farther and farther until I could no longer touch the sandy bottom. I clung to her waist, but she made me let go. She made me paddle and keep my head above water, swim a few feet away, ride up the side of waves, feel their height, and drop down on their backside in face of the next one. Fear never left me.

I was then made to venture over several waves alone. The water seemed like an older child, trustworthy only as long as it wasn't annoyed. I didn't know what would annoy it. I didn't know how to interpret its moves or how to avoid showing my fear, a show of emotion that would no doubt spur the demon into a bullying mode, or worse. And perhaps, I realized, that is what had happened the night before. Perhaps, as a group, we had shown too much of ourselves, our innocence and curiosity, our need to belong, our tribal tendencies. Perhaps all of it had swirled together without anyone paying attention to the rising mood that mounted and grew like a tidal wave bearing down on us as we looked the other way.

The evening before had started out innocently. All nine of us walked together, down a forbidden dirt road leading past the Russell farm and out to the huge sand dunes. We'd been instructed to follow a different road, one that took us first to Black Rock Beach then cut along the water to the dunes. But Paul said it was faster walking past the farm, and when we were out of sight of our house, we followed his lead.

The plan was to climb and roll and run down the high white dunes on the south side of the island during the last hour before sunset, before the mosquitoes came out in swarms. I was ten, Paul was eleven, my sisters were twelve, and Chuck was eight. Suzy, Bob, and Charlie were within the same age range.

We walked along, past the stone walls separating one field from the next, a herd of dairy cows, and a pond. Legend had it that a young, newly married woman had drowned in the pond, leaving her ghost to call wistfully for her husband and poke at the imaginations of the young.

"They say her hand reaches out of the water and pulls you in if you get too close," Paul warned in a loud, knowing whisper.

"No, sir," Chuck said with disdain.

"Yeah, it's true. Two kids fell in and drowned in that pond just a couple of years ago, and their brother swears he saw a hand pull them in."

I imagined the boys flailing in the water, snapping turtles and slime grazing their legs. But worse, I imagined the aloneness they must have felt in those moments when they dipped beneath the surface. It was a feeling I recognized as I was lifted by swells of the ocean tide, a feeling I tried to quell by looking for my mother or the bobbing heads of my brothers and sisters who swam nearby. I imagined those two boys, and I imagined them alone.

When Paul told that story the night before, the sun had just begun to set; he pulled out a pack of cigarettes. "I bet none of you have the guts to try one," he dared. "Just suck the smoke into your mouth. Watch." He expertly sucked in some smoke, held his jaws tight and his mouth round to form the smoke into rings as he blew it back out.

"Four," Lizzy had counted. "I can beat that."

I hadn't known Lizzy knew how to smoke, but when we all sat down at the base of a stone wall, each one of us occasionally rising up to look around to make sure no one could see us, Lizzy lit her own cigarette and blew rings while the rest of us giggled and passed them from hand to hand. As it was clear Lizzy had done this before, she quickly changed conversation while I marveled that all of us, including Chuck, were intent on trying the foul-tasting sticks.

"My father says these stone walls were built by slaves," Lizzy said.

"He says the early farmers had slaves working to clear the land, but that nobody wants to admit it 'cause the island is part of Rhode Island and Rhode Island is a liberal Northern state full of hypocrites."

"Yeah?" Paul asked, taking another drag from his cigarette while I coughed smoke out of my mouth. He seemed genuinely interested.

"Yeah. The farmers made a deal that if a slave could build a wall across the island he would be given his freedom. But nobody knows if anyone was ever able to do it, or maybe there was one, but there are more than three hundred miles of stone walls on this island and they sure as heck didn't let all those slaves go free."

"So they tricked them into doing the work?" Paul said.

"Yeah, I guess," Lizzy said.

"You know, this farm has been around since back then. The Russells are maybe the oldest family on the island or something like that," Paul said as he flicked the ashes of his cigarette over his knees.

"So they had slaves?" Lizzy asked.

"Yeah, probably. Don't you think?"

"I don't know," Lizzy answered. With dramatic flare, she flicked the ashes of her own cigarette and then, with an even more practiced pose, she took a long drag from between two fingers. The rest of us watched in awe, then Norma imitated her and Michael pulled another from the pack.

"You know old farmer Russell has got a haunted house. You can see it from the windows of our bedroom. It's pretty big," Lizzy volunteered.

"Probably had slaves build it. He's got about three or four houses back here and they're all his," Paul added.

"Yeah."

"How'd he get so many houses if he's the milkman?" Michael asked.

"I don't know."

"I do," Paul said. "I bet his grandfather or somebody had a bunch of slaves. That's how. I bet they made the slaves clear the land by building those walls and then they made them build the houses and they never let a single one of them go. Come on, let's go see that house." He jumped up and we all followed. The sun was setting in the western sky and the colors of the long rays over the fields had begun to grow strong.

None of us were looking for trouble as we stayed low next to the stone walls, but it started pulling at us like an undertow, and we got sucked into it fast—a huge wave of trouble that had crested but was still growing even as I swam high in the water that next day, looking for ways to get back to shore.

It started when Paul said we should stay hidden and the rest of us obeyed like trained animals. It felt as if we were playing Simon Says or a new version of hide-and-seek. It felt like a game. But something more was happening to me as we ran along bent beneath the tops of the stone walls in an effort not to be seen. I kept thinking about the slaves. I kept imagining how their hands would have been rubbed raw by the roughness of the boulders and their backs would have ached. And all the while, I couldn't separate my image of a slave from my image of Amelia. I couldn't separate the color of their faces or the shape of their bodies, and I realized for the first time that Amelia could have been a slave and that someone like Farmer Russell could have made her build a stone wall. And she would have had no choice. I squeezed my fingers into fists and continued to run, eager to keep up with the other children.

Paul had planted a reason to blame Farmer Russell for all slavery. By the time we reached the wall surrounding the empty house, a Victorian farmhouse with a door centered between double sets of windows, I was hating the man. I was hating the way my father treated Michael. I was hating that Amelia worked for us and was not part of the family. I was even hating the odd feeling of unfairness of being lucky enough not to be treated in these ways. The sun was setting directly behind the square frame and the two chimneys at either end of the house cast shadows like long, ominous spears.

"Are you sure this is a ghost house? It looks okay to me," Lizzy asked. I was glad when her voice broke into my thoughts. The rest of us whispered among ourselves about the uncut yard and the darkness inside.

"You don't think this is haunted? Do you see anyone in there? Do you?" Paul's voice rose an octave. "Look. Is there anyone in there?"

"Don't bust a gut," Lizzy snapped. "And, no, I don't see anyone, but it's not all run down, either."

"Not every single ghost house in the world is wrecked," Paul countered. "Here, throw this rock and we'll see if anyone comes out." Paul handed Lizzy a rock. She looked at Norma who nodded, then threw it gently against the side of the house. There was no response.

"See?"

"But you didn't throw it very hard," Norma interrupted. "Maybe they didn't hear. Maybe one of us should just go knock."

"Yeah, but who?" Michael asked.

"Forget it," Paul said. "I'll throw another rock." He picked up a small stone and threw it hard, really hard, and it crashed through a window next to the front door.

"You moron. What the hell are you doing?" Lizzy yelled.

"It doesn't matter. Nobody lives there. See? Nobody came out. Nobody will even know how that window got broken."

We all stood still, flabbergasted. Then a perverse kind of collective curiosity sucked straight into the wave of trouble heading toward us. Paul threw another rock and broke another window. "Hey, you guys, it's haunted. Nobody is going to care. Try it. It's really cool."

And we did. All of us. Over and over again. The double panes broke in unison, shadows of splintered glass visible in the shadows of its match. Rocks flew like tiny missiles and arms pumped with the fun of the spontaneity, the edginess, and the dare to see how fast we could break the windows, what patterns could be made in the process, and how large or small the rocks should be. We picked up and threw rocks as if what we were doing was as harmless as skipping pebbles on a pond, and we didn't stop until the sun had set and we couldn't see any reflection of light in the remaining shreds of glass. Every window in the house was broken. Some had been hit two or three times, some simply shattered on the first throw. Many were splintered; all of them were beyond repair.

"Holy hell!" Paul whistled. "We better get out of here."

"No kidding," Lizzy agreed, and we all waited her instructions. "Ok, everybody, let's get to the dunes. We'll run down once or twice, get sand all over us, then go home. We'll pretend we've been at the dunes the whole time. Agreed? Later tonight we swear an oath in blood."

"No, I hate that," Suzy yelled in protest. "I'm not gonna tell, but I'm not cutting my finger."

So we all agreed that blood oath or not, none of us would tell, and I forgot about the slaves as we talked in great excitement about what we'd done. It was not until we reached the driveway to our house that the possibility of real trouble sank in.

"Remember," Michael whispered, "nobody can tell. Chuck?"

"I won't."

"Mary?"

"No. I won't. But what if they ask? What if they see all those windows and they ask us if we did it?"

"They won't."

And so that night we were pulled to the top of the wave and over, left by ourselves to tread water on the backside and far enough away from what we had done to be able to drift into a restless sleep. By the next morning, each of us knew we would somehow have to get back to being ourselves, back to having a clear conscience. But we also knew, as we climbed down the cliff and spent the day on the beach, that a larger wave was bound to come crashing down, and that when it did, there would be punishment in its weight.

I thought about this as I worked to summon the courage to not only duck under the cresting water as I got closer to shore, but to choose which wave to ride. I then hesitated so long that I found myself watching my mother on the beach as she squeezed water from her hair and sat on the log poised like a lifeguard. I kept looking at Mama all the while being lifted by waves. Then I swam slowly forward, my head high so I could listen to Lizzy shouting to Michael. They knew which waves were curled for the best rides, so I tried to follow their lead with dread and wishful thinking. But I was farther out than they were, and missed the wave they rode while the one behind it slammed into my back.

Water filled my nose and mouth. The roaring and churning thrust me forward, sending my body tumbling. Down. I could do nothing. Down. I scraped my thighs and chin. Down. My bathing suit and hair filled with sand, and the undertow tried to drag me back as I dared to pull myself up. I stumbled forward and against that unmerciful pull, pushed, and got clear as the water drained back into the surf.

Breathlessly, having swallowed salt, sand, and foam, my bathing suit a weight between my legs, I reached the dry, small sand cliff and crushed the crisp surface of its wall. I walked up to the log where I wrapped a towel around myself like a cocoon and shivered as the heat of the sun penetrated the muscles of my shoulders. Mama pretended she hadn't seen me, perhaps sensing my shame—the shame that would wash over me in endless dreams of deadly waves—and calmly asked me, as she picked up the lunch basket, if I'd enjoyed my swim.

"Um," I answered.

"I was going to bring a thermos or two of fresh milk, but Farmer Russell didn't deliver any this morning, so I brought lemonade. I hope the milk will be there when we get home because I want to use the top cream on a blackberry cobbler tonight."

My shivering stopped. The others were still joyfully shouting and laughing in shallow pools, shaking the water from their hair, arguing about speed and size. I didn't dare move.

"You did pretty well out there. Those waves are very high today."

"But I scraped my legs."

"Not too bad. I saw your legs when you were walking up and I know they must sting, but once the salt dries, you'll be okay. And your chin is barely scratched."

"Yes, ma'am." I was glad she'd been watching and gingerly touched my chin to wipe away any sand, but then I couldn't help but wonder if she'd watched last night, too. I couldn't help but wonder if she knew what we had done but just wasn't saying, or maybe she was waiting for us to give ourselves away.

"Maybe we can have some milk with brown bread when we get home," I suggested, fishing for hints of her knowledge.

"Well, I told Amelia to watch for old Mr. Russell so she can put the milk straight into the ice box. Do you think Bob and Suzy are having a good time?"

"Yes, ma'am," I answered, relaxing a little in the change of subject. I wouldn't let anyone know how scared I'd been out in the waves and I wouldn't let them know how scared I was that we were the reason the milk had not been delivered. Instead, I looked out over the water and imagined the ships smacking against the rocks and the bodies of soldiers and Indians being thrown over the bluffs onto broken hulls. I pretended that I could swim as easily as the others and ride the waves as well as they rode bicycles or ate ice cream.

"You want some lunch?"

I nodded.

Later that evening, Amelia rubbed Noxzema on my sunburned shoulders, combed the tangles out of my freshly washed hair, and dabbed ointment on my chin and thighs. "The Lord want you out there swimming, he be giving you some fish gills," she muttered.

"Yes'm."

"And it ain't no wonder your daddy lit into you. You children deserve what all you got coming. What in tarnation did you think you were doing?"

I had no answer.

"I ain't seen your daddy that mad, nor your mama neither, ever. I ain't never heard nothing like what I heard—bunch of children knocking the glass out of somebody's home. Lord, almighty! And all you thinking you wouldn't get caught. You ever see a place where a bunch a children sit? Always something left behind. You think nobody would know who's shoes belong to you children? Farmer Russell didn't need to say nothing but bring me them shoes and me thanking him for finding them. And then him telling Mr. Bill about them cigarette butts and the windows. Lord Almighty, them windows."

"We didn't think anybody lived there."

"Why you think such a thing? Cause it ain't fancy? Your daddy says it's gonna cost nearly seven hundred dollars to fix all them windows. Seven hundred dollars. You think he got money like that to throw away?"

"What's going to happen?"

"I don't know. I surely don't know."

She rubbed the residue of Noxzema into her hands and I remembered the slaves whom my father said had built the stone walls. I imagined her building those walls, lifting the heavy boulders and positioning them one on top of the next, miles of back-breaking work. I imagined her hands, roughened and bleeding with the effort and her wide hips aching.

"Mimi, were you ever a slave?"

"No, child. Thank the Lord. But my grandparents were, and my daddy when he was a baby, but he didn't remember it none 'cept for the stories and the way there weren't no way for his daddy to make a real living."

"Did they have to move rocks?"

"I don't know. Why you askin'?"

"Just wondering."

"You best be wondering what kind of punishment you gonna get. That's what you be wondering about."

We didn't throw those rocks because the ancestors of Farmer Russell may have owned slaves. We didn't have any reason to do what we did, we simply were not thinking. We were acting as children will act when they join together in a group and allow themselves to go along. But the story of that night always reminds me that Amelia could have been a slave had she been born earlier, that she could have had to build the walls on Block Island. And it reminds me of the huge waves that so easily tossed me against the beach, and the stone walls that would one day symbolize the deep divide that separated me from my childhood.

In 1962, newspaper articles across New Jersey documented the high unemployment rates among African Americans and debated whether there were merits to keeping the schools segregated.

Smoke

MY FATHER SMOKED unfiltered cigarettes that crumpled when twisted between my small fingers. There was a camel on the package and mysteries promised in the exotic pyramids painted behind it. In those days, in the early 1960s, there was glamour in smoking. Truman Capote, Tennessee Williams, and others were photographed with mist-like clouds floating up from their cigarettes, which provided a sophisticated quality envied by lesser mortals. The women, bedecked in sequins and pearls, held long straw-like holders carved from ivory, whale bone, or hollowed jade, from which they delicately inhaled snake-like cords of smoke as they contemplated the world that idolized them. It was all about glamour and both my parents appreciated the art and skill behind its glory.

We had subscriptions to *Esquire*, the *New York Times*, the *New Yorker*, *Harpers*, and *Gourmet*. Weekly dinner parties frequently included artists, politicians, and authors. Nearly everyone smoked. Silver "silent butlers" with wooden handles and hinged tops were quietly used to empty ashtrays throughout the long evenings that started with martinis, gin and tonics, vodka on the rocks, or manhattans and ended with whiskey, port, and other liquors. There were manners involved in smoking and rituals—ways to hold a cigarette, ways to stub it out, to offer it to others, and to light it. Camels, Lucky Strikes, Pall Malls for men; Parliament or Kools for women; and Players to announce recent trips overseas.

Each morning, except Saturday, Amelia cleaned the many strategically placed ashtrays. On Saturdays this job was on my list of chores, and it was a filthy undertaking. Heavy, plate-sized crystal ashtrays or delicate china bowls marred with black burn marks and silky fine gray ashes were filled with cigarette butts despite the repeated emptying throughout the evenings. They smelled bad, like a combination of clothing that had soured mixed with heavy, wet metal. Sometimes the ashtrays held multiple kinds of filtered butts that had been stubbed out by Friday-night dinner guests, and sometimes they were full with only my father's unfiltered Camels. Regardless, when I dumped those butts in the garbage, the ashes flew up and, as I was still small, I had to turn my face away.

"Child, when you gonna learn to wipe 'em out 'stead of dumpin' 'em?" Amelia asked, handing me a rag.

Those Saturday mornings, my father drank black coffee and sat at the kitchen table reading the newspaper, mostly out loud, an odd and often irritating habit of his, while my mother and Amelia cleaned the dishes used by the many guests from the night before. They then made French toast or pancakes for our breakfast. My father didn't help. His hands were large, soft, and without calluses, but stained yellow-brown at the fingertips, and no one dared ask him to please go read somewhere other than in the middle of all the morning activity.

"Make sure you get them clean," he instructed me loudly over the newspaper, his head still bent to see the words despite wearing thick, black-rimmed glasses with Coke-bottle lenses.

"Yes, sir."

"Kathryn?" he addressed my mother.

My mother ignored him as she continued to whisk eggs.

"Did you see how these Northeast Democrats are pushing their high and mighty opinions on us? Hell, if you listened to Joe last night, he'd be happy to force integration like we're a Communist country." He sipped his coffee and lit his first Camel of the day. "Damn liberals will drive this country into the ground and it won't take much more than these next few years with Kennedy."

"Get your father an ashtray," Amelia whispered to me.

"Who the hell wants all this change? You mark my words, change the schools and no one will learn a thing."

I finished wiping out a small, three-legged molded ashtray from China as Amelia continued flipping pancakes that sizzled in hot browning butter.

"That's enough, Bill," my mother said, as if knowing whatever he said next would be ugly. She turned the water on in the sink, hard and loud.

Amelia put a plate of pancakes in the oven to keep them warm until we'd finished our chores, then took the vacuum out of the closet and left the room. I put the clean Chinese ashtray in front of my father, then returned to wipe the ashes from the scratches in a heavy crystal ashtray and was, as always, amazed that the sparkle reappeared after the abuse.

"Look here where there was a killing downtown," my father continued, still turning the pages of the *Trentonian*, a morning tabloid. "That's not happening in nice neighborhoods." He stubbed his cigarette out and drank his coffee. "And Kennedy wants to integrate? Change the schools? Change the neighborhoods so we can all get killed? I just don't get it. I've read studies that prove we have a higher level of intelligence. It's a hard fact, but it's a fact." He then lit another cigarette and let the smoke drift toward the ceiling while he continued turning the pages of the paper. "Liberals wouldn't make these decisions if they paid attention to the facts. But they don't. They don't want to know the facts."

I finished cleaning the last ashtray and asked to be excused. "Can I go now?"

"*May I please leave now*," he snapped.

"Yes, sir."

"Now ask your mother again."

"May I please leave now?"

"Go on upstairs and make sure your room is clean," my mother answered, "and tell Michael I need him to come take out the garbage. We'll have breakfast in about twenty minutes."

"Okay."

My father put down his paper. "How did you just answer your mother? You know you answer, 'Yes, ma'am.' You say, 'Yes, ma'am,' and you show some respect!"

"Yes, sir," I whispered. "I mean, yes, ma'am."

"Go on and get your room clean," my mother interrupted.

"Yes, ma'am."

"That's better." My father lit another cigarette. "Children around here aren't taught any manners." He resumed reading the paper, this time finding a local business story that was of interest to him. "Nobody with any manners. No sense, either."

I ran past Amelia in the living room, noting that she stood still while the vacuum cleaner groaned loudly. The room smelled of stale liquor and smoke. There were crumbs on the floor, a few dirty glasses and a napkin littering the table by the couch. She didn't seem to notice me. I hesitated, didn't say anything, wondered why she was so silent when she normally at least muttered her disagreements, shrugged, and continued upstairs where I told Michael that Mama needed him and that he better get down there 'cause Daddy was in a bad mood. Then I closed the door to my room, climbed on my bed, and stared out the window. *You are Southern!* A fact we were never allowed to forget.

Falling backward on my covers, I made a mental list of everything my father disliked. The school I went to. Schools in general. My friends. Anyone who wasn't Southern. The street we lived on. Northeastern liberals. Michael. Colored people. His mother. Most of the people he knew. Television. Children. Anything he read in the newspaper. Irish Catholics. Italians. Jews. His brother. Chattanooga, the city he was from. The nuns who taught us. Sports. Exercise. Kennedy.

He liked martinis. He liked to listen to the music of Broadway musicals. He liked my mother. And he liked to read. He imagined himself part of a sophisticated literary world—expatriates in Paris, Bloomsbury, the South. He read prodigiously—books were as necessary to him as water—and, as he lit one cigarette after another, he referenced the lives of the authors as examples of what was acceptable and what was not.

So I thought about the authors he was constantly quoting or using as examples of how one should behave—people who lived in the 1920s and 1930s, expatriates who wrote about a life of leisure, writing, talking, drinking, and dreaming. Those were the people he wished to emulate. He told us he could write, and that one day when he had time, he would write, and then he went on with the stories of bitter lives and grand debauchery. And as he spoke, he listed the charms of each character and their faults. He imagined himself one of them, a Gatsby or Jake Barnes.

Cigarette smoke wafted through the house. The vacuum cleaner was silent and my thoughts continued to drift. I wondered if my father liked Amelia. Was she separate from all the colored people he disliked? Did he really think she was incapable of learning? He'd never said anything about her specifically. He never said he liked her cooking or that she was helpful. He drove her to church on Sundays and made fun of her friends, but that was all. If he hated colored people, why was she living with us? Maybe it was Mama who liked her, but Mama never said anything either. By then, by the time I was ten, Amelia had been living with us five years and had worked for us the full twelve years since my sisters were born. Surely my parents must have liked her. Surely she was the exception to my father's long list of dislikes, but it was confusing. I loved her. I couldn't imagine not loving her, but I didn't think it was allowed.

I could smell the sweetness of cooking eggs braiding with the pungent aroma of Camel cigarettes. Voices rose in argument from Lizzy and Norma's room. The back door slammed as Michael took the garbage out. And it suddenly seemed odd that the scent of my father's cigarettes should be so strongly present in my room as he was downstairs in the kitchen.

I climbed off the bed and opened my bedroom door. The hallway was dark, but it was clear that the smoke was coming from the bathroom.

"Wait your turn," Chuck yelled between coughs, but the door wasn't locked so I entered the tiny room so full of smoke it was like white fog. Chuck sat on the bathmat in front of the tub with a silent butler half full of butts. He'd retrieved the longer burned stubs left over from the night before, stacked them alongside a silver lighter, and held a partially smoked Camel between his fingers.

"What are you doing? Are you crazy?" I waved my arms to try and clear the air.

Chuck answered between coughs. "Michael showed me how. Remember? Everybody does it. Are you gonna tell?"

"You're nuts. Breakfast is ready and Mama's gonna smell it on you."

"Naw. I just smoked Daddy's. Michael says everybody will think it's him."

"That's just stupid. Give me those," I said impatiently, grabbing the cigarette from his hand and stubbing it out in the bottom of the silent butler. I snapped the silver top closed with the lighter inside, deciding if I carried it downstairs I could pretend that I'd just picked it up from the debris left in the living room. I knew that later I would tell Amelia. I knew she'd make Chuck stop being stupid but that he wouldn't get into trouble—that the firmness of her hand would be used for soft caresses instead of slaps, that her intention to keep him from harm would take the edge from her words and turn them comfortable. And in that moment, I knew that we were lucky. I knew that no matter what my father said, we were lucky. That it didn't matter if he liked Amelia or not, she protected us from his harsh reactions and we were lucky.

As I walked through the house, the closed top of the silent butler kept the ashes from swirling and the foul, sour smell of stale tobacco from wafting. I didn't say anything as I walked past Mama, but she noticed and was glad I'd found it.

"I couldn't imagine where it was."

"It was on the floor by the couch," I lied as I handed her the lighter and dumped butts, still wet from Chuck's lips, into the empty garbage can.

"Well, get it clean," my father instructed sharply. "Chuck, sit down and eat your breakfast."

Once again, I wiped the ashes from a marred and burned surface, amazed by the sparkle beneath. Once again, I felt the grit of the ashes on my skin as the silver shined. And as I finished wiping, Amelia's hand reached down and took the container from me. A silent maid with the silent butler.

"The white man won't change easily," said Medgar Evers, field secretary of the NAACP. "Some of these people are going to fight hard. And more of our people could get killed." In June 1963 Evers was shot in front of his house hours after President Kennedy gave a speech calling for an end to violence.

———— ⤙⤚ ————

Prayers for Medgar Evers

AMELIA WAS MOVING slowly the way a black cloud sometimes moves against a blue sky, its energy mounting heavily with threatening rumbles and the occasional spilling of a venomous funnel.

"Ain't gonna be able to do nothin' 'bout it," she muttered, slamming the iron down on my father's shirt. "Ain't nothin' . . ."

"What ain't nothing?" Chuck asked, pushing his old yellow metal Tonka truck around on the brick red linoleum floor of the kitchen. He was bored by having to stay at home, and the toy, a remnant of his earlier childhood that no longer appealed to his eight-year-old self, was still easily available on the shelves behind the refrigerator.

"I ain't in no mood for your foolishness neither," she snapped.

It was as if lightning had struck. I stopped eating mid-bite and the hot cheese from my grilled sandwich dribbled down and burned my chin. Amelia never spoke sharply to Chuck.

"I ain't in no mood for nothing or nobody. Lord, can't be having nothing, no how. Ain't no use in . . ." The ironing board creaked with the force of her efforts. The muscles in her dark-brown arms tensed, contracted, and expanded. "Git up from off that floor, boy."

Mama insisted Amelia's "moments," as she called them, were none of my business and I wasn't supposed to ask what was causing them. But other moments had never felt so electric or scary as this one. And they were never directed at Chuck. No, Amelia's moments were usually directed at the Lord. She'd get herself worked up, slam pots and pans loudly in the kitchen or pull doors closed so hard the house shook, then ask the Lord what he was thinking, or why he didn't seem to "pay her no mind."

"Come on, Chuck," I whispered, picking up my plate to take to the back patio.

"Ain't 'come on, Chuck' time," she snapped at me. Again, like lightning. "You, Miss Priss, get on outside if you don't like being in here, but don't you 'come on, Chuck' that boy."

I sucked in my breath. It was as if time stopped while my mind raced forward with the knowledge that a thunderclap would follow or the hard strike of hail.

"Go on. Take that food with you and git on out. Go on, git."

Her words slapped. Still, I couldn't move other than to hang my head. It was worse than having hail pelting down on my back. It was as if Amelia had picked me up in a vile funnel and dropped me on the other side of the world. And I felt shame and confusion and fear all at once, a swirling combination that pushed me to a distance so far I didn't know how to move or how to get back.

"What'd she do, Mimi?" Chuck asked.

His voice reeled me in some, let air fill my lungs again, but Amelia slammed the iron down, and he, too, froze. "Didn't do nothing. Nothing. Just growing up and getting like all the rest of them. Hateful."

"Mimi?" I whispered, not recognizing her or the sound of my voice, yet meeting the realization that this outburst was not really directed at me nor at Chuck. Something had happened.

She turned to me, her face gleaming with beads of sweat and her glasses smudged. She sighed loudly with impatience and scorn, but with a note of apology. "Gone and lost my hat, that's what. Lost my hat going to that prayer meeting for Medgar Evers. Blowed right off and into the water and floated on down." The iron stayed flat on Daddy's shirt as Amelia looked up and out the window. Tears formed and dripped from the rim of her fat cheeks. Her breathing calmed between spasms and her elbows went slack against her side. The storm had passed.

"Who's Medgar Evers?" Chuck asked, his question like a clearing breeze.

"Man that died. That's who. And I was walking along by that river waiting on the meeting to start so we could pray for him and his family and the wind come up and takes my hat." Again she picked up the iron, stared at it as if she was no longer sure why it was in her hand, and then pressed it down. A moment later I could smell the cotton scorching.

"Mimi?"

She ignored me. "Ain't even lost my hat someplace where the Lord can find it knowing it belongs to me. No, I done lost it in the Delaware, that's what. Lost it some place ain't nobody knows me. Don't know that I come from near abouts the same place as Medgar and him being not so much younger than my Sylvester would'a been, and I'm hurting like I still lives there, hurting . . . 'cause that boy should'na died like that. And my boy . . ." She turned her gaze back to the ironing board and saw the scorch without concern. "And now I done lost," she began, then lowered the iron down onto the brown mark as if making sure it would remain.

Chuck and I looked at each other, trying to make sense of what she was saying. Her hat was important, almost as important as her Bible or the photo she had of her son, Sylvester, but I'd never heard the name Medgar Evers. The hat she put on every Sunday morning after pushing her large self into a heavily starched, floral cotton dress hemmed below her knees, thick stockings toned for white legs instead of brown legs, and black lace-up shoes polished to match the soft leather of her stiff, clasp handbag. The hat was the same black—bowler-style, with a straw weave and festooned with bright fabric flowers—and she pulled it down low to frame to her best features. She'd worn it each week to give glory on Sunday, the day she declared belonged to the Lord. The hat was what made me feel that our own church was somehow inferior or that the white members of the congregation were not as serious as the Negro members of Amelia's church because only very few wore hats.

Of course, I knew Sunday was the Lord's day, since by then I was in fifth grade at a Catholic school and had to go to Mass every week. At our church, however, as long as we had something on our heads it didn't matter so much if it was a hat or not. Some women used pieces of lace cut like triangles they kept stuffed in handbags. Some women even used tissues, which I found intriguing in that it seemed somehow so misguided and offensive when considering how important hats were at the First Baptist Church of Yardley, where they were used to help keep the Lord's attention. "Hats," Amelia had often explained, "help the Lord keep His eyes turned in my direction." So she always made sure her hat was worth looking at.

"Mimi," I began, as sympathy seeped into my hurt feelings like the whisperings of birdsong after a storm.

"Don't matter none."

"But Mimi, He'll see it. The Lord will know where it is so you can find it."

She didn't answer.

I thought about her hat, how it was always in pristine condition, and how she secured it to her hair each week with long pins. I realized I couldn't remember ever seeing her wear anything else on her head except her scarf, and I was suddenly afraid I might forget what Mimi looked like when she wore it, or that I would forget its smell, which I'd come to associate with the unpacked boxes in her room but was more likely the scent of the thick oil she rubbed into her scalp.

"Mama can get you another," Chuck suggested.

"It won't be the same," I whispered, despite a slight hesitation as I began to understand that her loss was not just the hat, "but Mama will get you a new one."

Amelia said nothing. I thought about how each week for the past several years, as she got ready for church, Amelia told Chuck and me— both of us pouting because she went happily without us—that the joy she felt was basking in the Lord's glory. I wondered. She'd start humming as early as Thursday afternoon, and by Thursday night she'd begin preparations for Sunday church and her day off on Monday. We'd watch her get ready, watch her silent, mounting excitement, all the while savoring her company and learning the meaning of bittersweet.

Who was Medgar Evers?

I thought about how Chuck and I would follow her up the stairs to her attic room, and how we would climb on her bed while she sat in her wicker rocking chair and took off her shoes. And then, while we got comfortable, we would inhale the musty scents of spilled rosewater and witch hazel wafting up from the ragged square of brown carpet tucked beneath the legs of her tiny bedside dresser and the metal wheels on the bed frame. We'd feel the sprinklings of the baby powder she'd dusted in her shoes—tiny white particles that had floated through the air to reflect the sun's rays before landing on her bed—and we would rub our fingers over the traces of Vicks Vaporub coating her sheets. It wasn't a clean room. There were no clear surfaces or empty corners. Nothing shone. Dull colors and faded materials in a crazy quilt she used for a spread showed old spots of spilled juice and ineffective scrubbing. No, it wasn't a clean room, but there was comfort in it—a deep, calming comfort that enveloped me each time I climbed the narrow steps with Chuck.

We'd sit on her bed and chat aimlessly about homework, games we played after school, and sibling arguments, and sometimes while we spoke Amelia's eyes misted. Sometimes she put her head back on the chair and rocked just enough to regain her energy or close out the day. I never knew which, and thinking about it, I didn't know if Chuck noticed or if he was too young. But I did know that maybe the comfort I felt sitting up in what my mother called "the chaos, her room," was really maybe no comfort for Amelia at all. And that thought hit me square between the eyes as I visualized her holding her hat on her lap, pinning the flowers to it or mending the ribbon. Maybe her room was just a place for her to store parts of the person she had once been, or the person she was when she went to church on Sunday, or the person she wanted to be, and maybe that person wasn't somebody we knew anything about. Like Medgar Evers.

There were stacks of unopened boxes lining the walls of that attic room and they were covered with dust and crayon markings, all holding evidence of an earlier life. There were mimeographed church flyers smeared with ink, folded unevenly, littering the limited floor space and announcing activities we knew nothing about. There were pill bottles of every shape and size cluttering the bedside table, and old-smelling castor oil she used for mysterious ailments. Everything in Amelia's room was evidence that she had a life I knew nothing about, a life that made her smile as she started getting ready to leave us each week, a life she no doubt preferred.

"Ain't no need for me to clean up that room if I'm only gonna sleep in it," I once heard her snap at my mother. "Not enough time in the day for me to want to fool with it."

Sometimes while we were up there, snuggled together under the musty quilts, Chuck and I could hear my father yelling at Michael and I'd fight the urge to crawl under the bed or disappear into a dark corner. Hide. Cover my ears. And I'd look over at Amelia, steady myself with her presence, and feel Chuck inch closer to me.

"Gonna tell me a story from the Bible tonight?" Amelia would ask, interrupting the anxiety expanding in my chest. She'd pick up the worn black book splayed open on the box by her side. Her swollen fingers with close-clipped fingernails would smooth down the thin ribbon used to mark her page, and she'd hand it to me with a tired smile. The voices downstairs would fade as I opened to the colored pictures of Joseph sawing wood or meadows full of flowers. Chuck would sometimes let his head drop onto my shoulder.

It was always easy to tell the stories of Adam and Eve or Cain and Abel. It was even easier to describe a wicked pharaoh or sinful mothers, but I never wanted to do so.

"Which story you gonna read?" I'd ask instead, handing the Bible back to her.

Amelia never said anything about the fact that she couldn't read. She followed words with her finger and uttered memorized prayers or phrases. Her favorite was Psalm 23, which she'd embellish to describe the green pastures and the still water. "Like the Delta," she said. "Like that." I didn't really believe she couldn't read, but Daddy said she couldn't, said she'd never had any education and was probably better off. I didn't know what he meant. I didn't know what any of it meant.

Amelia said she'd make an X so she could vote, but it wasn't enough as she wanted to know how to write and she didn't like the idea that an X would become her last name. She liked her name: Amelia MacIntosh. She said it sounded strong and she didn't think she'd give it up for an X even if she agreed with the preacher who said that it might be a good idea. To vote. To sign her name. To change her name to X.

"But it ain't right," she'd said. "Only right is to get some learning, learn how to sign my name. That's the only right way. Let them children get some schooling, real schooling."

Did she know she was teaching us?

Often while we were in her room, I visualized reeds growing up from mud flats, a basket with a baby in it floating in shallow water, and heat shimmering over everything. The shouting downstairs would eventually stop, and the house would grow quiet. Amelia would let her finger rest on a paragraph in the middle of a page and close the cover of the Bible, as if she'd been reading, as if we wouldn't remember from one week to the next that the words and details changed. She'd put the Bible on her bedside table and sometimes hand a tin full of her plastic white snap beads to Chuck, and then tell us about Sylvester. While she talked, Amelia gathered her hat, checked the ribbon around the brim over and over again, and changed the position of the flower. There never seemed to be enough time before Mama called us back downstairs to go to bed, so I was always anxious to see how the hat would look, which flower would be used, which way Amelia would call on the Lord's attention.

She owned three flowers, each rewrapped on Mondays after Miss Ruth, her friend from church, brought her home, each tucked in tissue paper at the bottom of the hat box.

"I know Miss Ruthie thinks my hat is too plain," she said, "but Lord, that woman, sweet as she is, puts things on top of her head meant only for a donkey to eat. Now my Sylvester always did love this hat, so as long as I can make it look presentable, this will be the hat I wear until my dying day. My Sylvester, he said this hat made me look like a movie star. Sweet child. He was a sweet child."

Amelia only once told us what happened to Sylvester, only once described the night he was running a high fever and coughing like his chest would split. She'd given Peter all the money she'd saved hidden in the folds of two shirts he never wore, knowing he wouldn't think to look for it in his own clothes. She said when Sylvester's coughing wouldn't stop she shook those shirts and let the money drop right out—didn't care if Peter used every penny as long as he got her child some medicine to stop his coughing. Only Peter didn't do what he was supposed to do. Peter ran off with that money, and drank it. He found a woman for the night and let Sylvester die.

My stomach hurt when Amelia told me that. She said her son, her baby, her only child, died in her arms as the first morning light cast gray shadows in his room. Peter barged through the front door—too drunk to lie down, too drunk to know that Amelia's life had drained away with Sylvester's, too drunk to care.

"Never let that man touch me again," she'd whispered. "My Sylvester passed because of him. Peter said it wasn't his fault. Said my child had bad blood and there weren't nothin' . . . but Sylvester didn't have no bad blood. No, sir! He did not! Now I knows the Lord giveth and the Lord taketh away, but seems like Peter done pushed things along weren't meant to be pushed." She took off her glasses and let her hands drop to her lap on either side of her hat. "And he was only a lamb. Child was only twelve. Just turned. An innocent." Her voice softened to a low hum and the room became silent, like swimming under water. "Weren't no call, weren't no reason." Her fingers then fluttered over the fabric flowers, and then, as if drawing strength through her hands, she smiled slightly. "Boy loved this hat."

"It was a beautiful hat," I finally whispered to her, the steam from the iron still sizzling.

"Um hum," Amelia agreed, her energy gone and the room silent. She never again spoke about her son, her hat, or Medgar Evers.

By 1963, as the means to enforce laws to integrate schools were being debated, the number of violent clashes between blacks and whites in New Jersey began to rise.

The Turning Point

"THE ONLY REASON they live in the city is so that her father can get votes—Catholic votes and Negroes," my father sneered as he began a familiar diatribe. We'd barely left the house and, as he pulled our wood-paneled station wagon out of the driveway, he was already making sure I knew he didn't approve of Kathy becoming my friend. I bit my bottom lip and tried not to listen. I knew. He'd already told me.

Mama was busy getting the house ready for her Friday-night dinner party. She'd asked my father to drive me to Kathy's house, and I didn't know if he was mad because he had been interrupted from reading or because he didn't like Kathy's father. He didn't say much but stared at me through his thick glasses as he banged the door to the car.

Kathy's father was an Italian state senator. My father insisted that it was important to know he was both—Italian and a state senator—as his family's heritage explained why he was Catholic, and the fact that he was an Italian Catholic explained why he was a liberal democrat. For these reasons, according to my father, I was to understand that we did not agree with Kathy's father's politics.

"Liberal democrats want to change the schools so the Negroes can get the same education you get even if they don't learn anything. Hell, we've already given them their own teachers. And don't you think for one minute that just because they can read and write they are qualified to do anything. Brown versus the Board of Education didn't do anything to change that. That was just a lot of politics without facts. You ever see one of them even bothering to keep their own house clean? Look at the way they move in and let whole neighborhoods fall apart. You'll never see them doing anything more than shining shoes and or driving delivery trucks, but they'll feel educated and we'll be paying for it."

It was the sound of his hatred that scared me, the way his words vibrated like the twang of a cold metal saw with sharp teeth, each point threatening to tear away another small piece of the innocence his audience may have had. I pushed his words away, but they drifted in and out of my thoughts. I looked out the car window in search of brown children who might be starting at my school and glanced fearfully to check his expression to know whether he suspected. His thick glasses never turned in my direction. He didn't know that I would make friends with children with brown skin, or that the flipside of his hatred gave me hope—hope that with integration the walls he tried to create would crumble and I would meet more people like Amelia.

We drove for nearly twenty minutes toward Trenton while he continued his tirade about schools and Negroes. Then, as the streets became more populated, his focus expanded and he began making jokes. There were all kinds of people out on the sidewalks, new targets for his mocking—fat people; people who wore clothes he didn't like; men who walked with their heads down or their hands in their pockets; women who didn't wear the right kind of hat or wore too many different colors; people whose skin was slightly dark; and, as always, Negroes. He believed he was hilariously funny.

Disappear, I thought. *Me or him.*

It didn't matter to me if Kathy was Italian, I liked the way she skipped rope and laughed at the same time. She was short and had wide hips and a square shape—so unlike my skinny, tall self that we giggled at our differences. I liked that she got good grades and that the nuns called on her to answer all the questions in science and math. And I liked that when I'd read aloud stories we'd been assigned to write, she always said mine were best. We were becoming good friends. My father's voice faded.

Finally, he pulled to the side of the curb in front of a large brick house perched on top of a steep hill. Late October rain had knocked lingering leaves from huge trees and had left puddles everywhere. The wide brick steps up to the front porch were wet, brownish-red, gleaming, and slick, and they were beautiful, enchanting, somehow majestic, enticing in their offer of escape.

"I'll be back to get you at five o'clock," my father said from behind the steering wheel, his voice changed to anger again. "Wait for me on the porch and come down when you see me. I don't want to have to climb up all those stairs."

"Yes, sir," I answered as I pushed open the door. Two hours.

Five o'clock. It would be dark by then. Wishing I could stay longer, I swooped down to pick up a few of the fallen leaves. Water dripped from their orange and yellow skins. It ran down my hand, my wrist, and into the sleeve of my thick wool sweater. Shaking it off, I remembered how Kathy and I had tied dry stems together at recess on the playground. We'd made necklaces and crowns, flattened them between the pages of our textbooks, and rubbed them like wood blocks with our crayons. *These stems will be easier,* I thought, feeling how pliable the wetness made them. *We could do a lot in two hours. . . .*

Quickly climbing the brick steps, I assumed my father was watching and as I reached the entrance to the porch, I turned to wave good-

Mary M. Barrow

bye. The car was gone. *Always wait,* he'd said a thousand times. *A gentleman always waits until the person is inside before leaving. That way you know they are safe.* I shrugged. *Disappear. Me or him.* Did he create these feeling intentionally? Did he do this on purpose?

The front porch was deep and spanned the full width of the house. Unpainted wicker rocking chairs padded with thick cushions lined the walls and crowded the corners. The chairs were stained but inviting. It was easy to imagine the fun we would have sitting with our feet curled under us while we wove the leaves into long chains and knitted twine. There were low tables covered with chalk and crayons, beckoning me like a moth to light, while beneath them the floor was littered with toys and puzzle pieces. The porch of Kathy's house was like a child's wonderland, and despite the nagging suspicion that Mama would have had a fit about the mess, already the promise of two wonderful hours was being fulfilled.

I knocked on the door and within seconds Natalie, Kathy's older sister, opened it. "Mom's not home and I'm in charge. You have to do what I tell you," she announced.

I nodded, grateful for the added adventure of not having an adult around, and followed her into the house.

Natalie was big for her age—overweight and tough. But not *mean* tough. Tough because she was big, and in the Catholic school we all attended, anything out of the normal range was a reason for being teased. While my height had just begun to attract attention, Natalie had been teased for years. She took it, stood her ground, but remained fair-minded and kind. I admired her kind of toughness.

Kathy, a smaller version of Natalie, was in the kitchen, a room even more enticing than the porch. It was full of art projects. There was a Popsicle-stick house under construction on top of a cardboard box; a half-finished oil painting leaning against the wall; watercolors and crayon drawings framed or tacked over the counters; and clay bowls of different sizes drying on the top of the refrigerator, on the breadbox,

152

and on the window sills.

"Do you want to draw or something?" Kathy asked, as Natalie handed me a glass of milk and a huge chocolate brownie. "I have to watch my little brothers, 'cause dumb Nattie says she has to do her homework. But they won't bother us." Natalie shrugged her shoulders and left the room while their two younger brothers flicked paint at each other.

"Cut it out," Kathy shouted.

I smiled. I liked being there. I liked how familiar it felt and yet how different it was. I liked that as I watched and looked around I knew my mother would probably like it, too, despite the mess.

"Our mothers know each other," Kathy announced as if reading my mind.

"They do?"

"Yep. They paint together. Same as us. They paint the stuff that goes on the stage at the Children's Theater. You know, the scenery. Didn't you know that?"

"Nope."

"Yeah, well I guess your mom has to 'cause she's the president of the Junior League and that's what they do."

"No, it isn't. She talks on the phone and gets everybody to go to meetings."

"Well, I don't know, but my mom says your mom is a really good artist."

I nodded, knowing only that my mother sometimes sketched.

We made a mess that afternoon with finger paints and pottery, and the time passed with the new security that came with knowing that our mothers were friends, and that a kind of destiny between us was therefore inevitable.

It was nearly five o'clock and my two hours passed when we all decided to play hide-and-seek. I hid once under the dining room table, once in the back stairwell from the kitchen up to the bedrooms, and then in a closet with a huge raccoon-fur coat that must have belonged to their father, the state senator. The boys ran in and out of the front door, the noise of their excitement bouncing around the house like a deflating balloon.

I was so absorbed in having fun, in the feeling of freedom and the excitement of our new friendship, that I didn't at first realize anything was wrong. I was hiding behind the heavy drapes in the dining room, waiting for Kathy to find me, when I heard voices I didn't recognize. Then I heard the boys run into the house and I could hear Natalie telling them not to come back out. She wasn't kidding. She wasn't playing. Her voice had a tone I'd only heard once before when Amelia shouted for me to stay still as a car barely missed hitting me while crossing the road. I peeked from behind the drapes.

Natalie was still on the porch, and there were other girls there, too.

"Kathy, call Mom," she yelled, loudly.

Kathy must have deserted her own hiding place as I heard her pick up the rotary phone. I heard a much deeper voice from the porch shouting that Natalie had called her a "black bitch and a nig—"

I pushed the drapes away and tiptoed to the front door. Natalie was alone, in the center of three older and much larger African American girls.

"What'd you call me?" the largest of the three was asking. "What'd you call me?"

"I didn't call you anything," Natalie answered, firmly but without anger.

The girl swung her arm and hit Natalie on the side of the face. "Somebody's been calling me names. You white bitch living up here, thinking 'cause you rich and you white you can call me names?"

"No."

A second girl hit her.

I screamed loud, as loud as I could, but I didn't go out on the porch and they looked at me, then hit Natalie again before they ran, jumping down the front stairs and laughing. Kathy was shouting into the phone for her mother to come home. Natalie stood stunned until I opened the door and she walked in and sank down into a chair.

I could still see those girls. They were laughing as they ran down the hill instead of using the enchanted brick stairs and then they were gone. Still, their shouting voices echoed as Natalie touched her face and winced. Her cheek was swelling on one side and her eye was closing on the other. I moved forward to go to her, to sit next to her.

"Are my brothers alright?" she whimpered. "Ask Kathy if they're okay. I'm supposed to be in charge. I'm supposed to take care of ..." Her hands started shaking. "Tell them to stay in the kitchen."

I was amazed she wasn't crying.

"Tell them to stay there until my mom gets home."

I opened the door just as Kathy pushed past me. "You do it," she said to me as she went out to Natalie. "You be in charge of the boys. I'll get Band-Aids ... my mom is coming ... she's coming. And she called the police. The police are coming, too."

"Okay," I answered, relieved to be told what to do, relieved that I knew her mother was coming as I turned toward the boys.

They stood in the hallway looking like startled deer. "Come on, let's go," I instructed, leading them back into the room full of art and imagination. The younger pulled the other's hand and they both crawled under the table. I wanted to join them but I also wanted to be with Kathy, so I stood in the doorway and I watched as she brought Natalie into the living room and got her to sit on the couch.

I'd never seen such love between sisters. Kathy held her hand under Natalie's elbow. She kicked aside a toy then leaned forward while still holding Natalie so that she could place a cushion to provide support as she helped her sister to sit. Natalie let her do everything. It was as if she'd relinquished her position of being the eldest, as if she knew unquestionably that she could trust her younger sister to take care of her.

Then just as suddenly as everything else that had happened, my father was standing in the frame of the front door. For a moment, just a moment, there was a collective relief in seeing him and our fear began to evaporate as words spewed, shaking, from our scared selves. The boys came out of the kitchen and joined the chorus of telling.

My father, however, stood where he was. He barely came inside, and never changed his expression. He hushed us all and then asked Natalie, without going to her, if she was okay. She nodded, although her hands were clasped tightly together and there were tears streaming down her swollen face.

"Well, then, we can go," he said to me. "Their mother will be here in a few minutes."

"But shouldn't we wait?"

"She says she's okay, so there's nothing for me to do. She's okay."

Everyone in the room became still, completely silent. I looked from Natalie to Kathy and then to the boys. None of them looked at me or at my father. No one moved.

We shouldn't leave. We shouldn't leave them alone.

"It's alright," Natalie said, her voice taking on the toughness she reserved for the bullies at school. "You're right, there is nothing you can do. I'm fine."

"No," I said, stepping forward, my fists clenched beside me. "No, we should wait."

"Young lady," my father hissed, his voice sharp and steely. "Go get in the car."

My breath caught in my throat. I'd never spoken back to him. Terror. I swallowed it. "What if those girls come back?" I asked with less daring, my voice shaking.

Kathy wrapped her arm around her sister's shoulder. She gave me an odd look, and I understood in that instant that she was terrified and if we left I would lose her friendship. It didn't matter how much older Natalie was or how often she insisted that she was okay; I knew we should stay until her mother got home and I knew my father was not doing what an adult should do.

"We should stay."

"Go get in the car, now!" he repeated.

"But the police are coming. We should stay!" I shouted, a new kind of anger surging through me.

My father grabbed my wrist and pulled me out the door; there was nothing I could do. But he'd created something in me that wasn't there before, something that felt both hollow and heavy.

"Get in the car! We need to get home. Your mother is expecting us home for the party and Natalie is fine," he hissed at me. Then he turned back to Kathy and Natalie. "The police will probably be here in a minute. You tell them what happened and I hope they find those girls, but I saw them running in all directions when I got here, so I don't think they'll get caught. Nothing I tell the police will help, so there is no use in me staying. It all probably has something to do with your father being a senator."

Natalie didn't answer. Kathy's eyes squinted with anger and I saw her take the hands of both her brothers and pull them to sit with her and Natalie.

I couldn't speak and I couldn't remember going down the beautiful brick stairs that had brought me so close to this friendship. By blaming the attack on their father, my father had just compounded the insult of not staying. How could he? How could he believe it had anything to do with their father? It was random and it was stupid. It was bullies out for kicks. And it had nothing to do with Natalie or with Kathy. But Natalie was hurt and my father didn't stay with her—my father didn't care, and he didn't do what a father should do. He never did. He never, ever helped. And I didn't know why. We were children, but even a child knows when help should be given.

All I could think as he drove me home was that I wished I, too, had been punched so that maybe he would have understood how bad it was for Natalie. Maybe then he would have thought about our terror.

But then I remembered he hadn't waited to see if I got safely into the house. He didn't watch and he didn't care. He wouldn't have cared if I had been the one punched, and he wouldn't have acknowledged that it was anything unusual.

"So now their father will see that even senators don't get a pass from those animals," he said as I stared incredulously at him, his thick glasses reflecting the headlights of passing cars and his hands gripped loosely around the steering wheel. My chest tightened around the hollow weight.

I went straight to my room. My father didn't try to stop me, and my mother didn't come to check on me. Perhaps she didn't know, or he hadn't told her everything, but it didn't matter. I stood in front of the mirror, trying and failing to hit myself in the face while their dinner party proceeded as if nothing had happened.

Congestive heart failure is often a complication of syphilis.

A New Kind of Dying

IT WAS LATE, dinnertime. My stomach rumbled and my hands ached from my after-school piano lesson held in the little window-encased porch room attached to the side of the convent by my school. I couldn't read the notes in the music books, and the nun who taught me was easily aggravated. That day, I could hear the whacks she gave when the student before me missed the timing in her songs, and knew the assault on my fingers would be compounded by my slow learning. The tension was so thick that it was difficult to imagine that the room was part of the house where God's servants ate and slept. I hoped for some grave crisis to interrupt us. Instead, when my lesson was over, I was simply glad my mother was late picking me up as it allowed me time to sit on the steps and rub the welts on my fingers where the nun had whacked them with a ruler after every mistake.

Inhaling deeply and pulling the cuffs of my sweater down, the wait gave my eyes time to dry, and the November cold turned my hands red enough to camouflage my shame. I didn't want anyone to know how little skill I had when sheets of music were pushed in front of me, as I found great joy in sounding out songs and improvising without the squally little black notes.

When the station wagon finally came around the corner, the sky had turned purple and rain clouds had moved overhead. The dusk had faded to dark and there was even less of a chance that my signs of failure would be noticed. I relaxed.

It was surprising, however, to see both my parents in the car. As I climbed into the backseat, Mama handed me an apple. Her clothes smelled of cooking. My father drove. Without greeting, he explained we'd be stopping by the doctor's office on the way home.

"Nothing about you," my mother interrupted, turning back toward me with a reassuring smile.

We listened to the radio, to the news. My father said something about how it was criminal to use so much of our tax money to pay the secret service so Kennedy could gallivant around the country. "What the hell does he think he's going to do in Texas?"

He hated Kennedy and ranted about him endlessly. Arguments at dinner parties had grown toxic as he insisted Kennedy was leading us into a war in Vietnam and that nobody wanted to see how corrupt his whole administration was because he was young. My father's hatred was so tangible it became easy to dismiss his views. I only knew that the nuns at school had us praying for Kennedy to win the election. And then after he won, we were praying for Jackie, and their children's happiness, right alongside praying for the departed soul of Pope John and the souls of the pagan babies in purgatory. We memorized Kennedy's speech, "Ask not what the country can do for you, ask what you can do for the country," and we saluted his picture, which was next to the flag in many of our classrooms. Kennedy could do no wrong during the school day, and no right when home at night.

More importantly than the opinions of the nuns or my father, however, was Amelia's. Amelia liked him. She didn't say much about him—

didn't dare—but she liked watching him. She'd turned on the news at night, which was a new habit, and she nodded in agreement whenever he said something about equal rights. My father's views became background noise.

"What's he going to do? Hang around a barbeque pit?" he continued as we drove toward the doctor's office. "Texas oil money may like him now, but they will grow tired of Boston liberals. The whole trip—Houston, San Antonio, Dallas—it's a complete waste of money—tax payers' money."

Mama didn't say anything. She rarely said much about politics, but she seemed distracted, and I wondered if she felt bad and if we were going to see the doctor about her.

The waiting room was small with a few chairs and a stack of worn magazines in a corner stand. No one else was there. I remember the hidden pictures in *Highlights for Children* were already circled; the one *Jack and Jill*, with a cover featuring Rin Tin Tin, had half the pages torn out. It wasn't worth reading. The walls of the room were a dull yellow, a color that at one time was meant to soothe, but had aged badly and was now ugly. A steam-clanking radiator, covered in thick, peeling paint, stood between the two windows and released small belches of sour-smelling fog.

My parents had barely walked through the door when the doctor in his white coat motioned for them to follow him into his office. Mama told me to wait quietly, so I reluctantly settled in the one vinyl-covered chair that was pushed up against a low, stained, cloth-covered couch. Having quickly noted the condition of the magazines, I searched through the loose papers in my book bag. Crushed beneath my piano books and the half-eaten bread pretzel I'd bought earlier in the afternoon—a nickel every Thursday to help raise money for the pagan babies—was a mimeographed list of spelling words. Smoothing the creases in the paper out on my lap, the ink smeared on my hands and added a purple hue to my red, sore fingers.

As I sat waiting, I could hear their voices but not their words. The spelling list seemed harder than usual. I tried to concentrate, but outside the window I could see the wet road reflecting the headlights of rush-hour traffic. If I squinted, the streams of light on the pavement seemed to float. I remembered the painting we looked at in our art books— *The Scream* by Edvard Munch, which Sister Gertrude had suggested we copy during art class. Some of the other children thought it was creepy, and maybe it was, but there was something about it. I looked away from the window and I got to the first letter of the third word on the list, C for "celebrate." C-e-l . . . Christmas was in a few weeks and I wondered what I would get. Mama's voice sounded strange in the doctor's office.

It was by chance that I was there with my parents, and by chance that I would be privy to their conversation as we drove home. Mama kept her face mostly turned toward the window, but my father couldn't stop talking, his voice actually choked despondently, wavering between disgust, disbelief, and anger.

"And she is the most God-fearing, pious person I've ever known," he said. "That son of a bitch."

"Don't," my mother whispered, motioning with her head to remember I was in the car.

"How long did he say she's had it? Must be years. Years. Probably since they were first married. Or maybe he picked it up later. Didn't he tomcat around? Didn't she tell you how he came home most nights drunk? Didn't she tell you that?"

"Shhh . . ."

I had no idea who they were talking about, but they clearly were not talking about my mother, so I didn't pay much attention at first. Instead, I frantically tried to pull my uniform sweater arms down to cover my hands, as they were cold and still stinging. I wanted to at least wash the ink off before anyone noticed the marks.

"We're not going to tell her," my mother said in an emphatic whisper, then turned her head again to the window. "There is no earthly reason for her to know at this late point."

"That's right. You're right. No, we won't tell her. We won't tell her. We'll tell her she's got herself tired out or that her heart is tired, no cause for alarm and the pills are to help build up her energy."

They were both silent. I knew not to say anything, although I had by then guessed they were discussing Amelia. Whatever they were saying was more serious than my hands or Kennedy's trip to Texas, but it seemed like they had a plan and that Amelia would be all right.

"Said he might have got it while he was in the army. Wasn't he in . . . wasn't he . . . good God, has she seen him during her vacations? I didn't think . . . well, no, she would have had to have this much longer than four or five years. That's what it's been, hasn't it? About five years, since I put him back on the train?" my father said.

Again, they were both quiet. My father drove slowly, like he was giving himself time before we got home.

"Not a single word. Ever. It would break her heart," my mother whispered.

"Mama?" I had to ask.

"This is nothing to do with you, young lady. Nothing."

"Yes, ma'am."

My father sighed. "Whatever you think is best." He rubbed his fingers over his lips. "I know he was in the army," he continued, "but I don't think he went overseas. Stayed mostly in Alabama, I think. I think he might have been too old. Hell, if she is sixty-two now, he'd be about eighty, so when the war ended, he must have been near on sixty. He must have been lying. Hell, he lied about everything. Course, maybe he didn't know how old he was. Wasn't like the army was going to check."

Neither spoke.

"He could have had it before they got married. Hell, he could have got it anytime. And they say it gets passed on. They say . . . you don't think she had it when . . ."

"Hush. Just hush!" my mother's voice cracked.

"Well, do you think she could have had it then? She says that boy had all kinds of trouble—hearing and his teeth."

"I don't know, and I don't want to know." Mama sounded as if she would cry.

Daddy's voice dropped. "Died of pneumonia . . ." He turned on the windshield wipers. "Son of a bitch. Stupid son of a bitch. There's been penicillin for it for years, years. Since the late forties. If he got it in the army, even if he got it before they got married, all he had to do was go to the damn doctor and get some penicillin."

"I'm telling you to hush. We don't know what happened and we're never going to tell her. Nobody should know this. It would shame and embarrass her. We're not saying another word."

Mama's face was wet despite an ironclad resolve in her voice.

I knew they were talking about Amelia. I knew the minute Daddy said he'd died of pneumonia. Only person I've ever heard of dying of pneumonia was Sylvester. But I couldn't put it all together.

"I'm just trying to figure it out," Daddy started up again. "Figure out how long she might have had it."

"What difference does it make? She's got it. It's all though her whole body and there is nothing that can be done about it. So we let her be. That's it. We let her be."

A few minutes later, we were home. The dogs were barking and Michael was yelling at Elizabeth to get out of his room. I could smell the fried chicken that Mama's sweater had hinted at, and Amelia was mashing potatoes.

"Get your coat off and help me set the table," Amelia said to me. "Tell your mama this will be ready in just a few minutes."

I happily dropped my coat on the floor of the hall closet. My stomach was rumbling. She turned toward me and inspected.

"Wash your hands first. I made your favorite potatoes—mashed with cream."

I told myself that whatever worries my parents had about Amelia were wrong. She was fine. Dinner was ready and the house was warm. I washed my hands and let the water run over the tiny cuts from the ruler's edge. I decided that if Mama noticed I could say it was just chapped skin from the cold, or maybe I scraped them on the school wall while I was at recess.

Mama didn't notice, but later that night Amelia rubbed Vaseline over them, her broad, brown hands holding mine carefully, gently.

The next day my spelling test was canceled. The whole school was called into the auditorium. Sister Gertrude was crying so hard she could barely tell us what had happened. Kennedy had been shot. He was dead.

Amelia's heart was broken.

The Tuskegee Institute was founded in 1881 by Booker T. Washington as a school for colored teachers. Under Washington's leadership, it became nationally and internationally known for excellence.

In 1941, in an effort to train black aviators, the U.S. Army established a training program at Tuskegee Institute.

The Tuskegee syphilis experiment was conducted between 1932 and 1972 by the U.S. Public Health Service to study the natural progression of untreated syphilis in poor, rural African American men who thought they were receiving free health care from the U.S. government.

Peter and the Railroad

1964

JANUARY ICE FORMED around windowpanes with tiny lines like spiderwebs reaching toward the center. There were thick blankets on Amelia's bed and the room was slightly steamy with menthol scents from the open jar of Vicks Vaporub. I guessed Amelia had a cold, but she wasn't coughing or sneezing, and at age eleven I couldn't imagine much beyond a sore throat.

"Jump down a minute so I can get my feet up on them pillows I got under the covers," she instructed. Chuck and I were sitting next to her on her bed snapping plastic pearls together. We both got off and she pulled back the blankets.

"Here now, child, put them pillows under my ankles." She hoisted her legs up by pulling on the fabric of her nightgown. "Lord, they is sore today." Her ankles had lost their shape. They were stretched and translucent, like brown balloons.

"How come they're swelled up like that?" I asked, pushing the pillows into place, unconcerned, unable to imagine the discomfort, and unwilling to leave the story she'd started telling us about Peter working on the railroad. "Did Peter have ankles like that?"

She almost laughed at the thought and her face softened for a moment. "Lord, no," she answered, as she pulled the blankets back over her legs. "That man was so skinny I could have stood him up next to a telephone pole and he would have plain disappeared. Child, my Mr. Mac was so tall he made me look like a big ol' jelly-filled doughnut. You know, like them new ones we gets from the Bond Bread man." She shook her head, a smile still lingering at the corners of her mouth. Chuck climbed back on the bed and I followed. "Careful now. Don't let them beads roll off the sides," she warned, then winced when one of us hit the covers over her legs. "Careful."

It was strange for Amelia to be in bed, but it felt like an adventure. She used the free time to tell us stories about her past, something she did infrequently. And that night as she leaned forward, rubbing her legs beneath the blanket, I listened carefully to her stories.

"No, child, Peter didn't have no swollen ankles, didn't have no swollen nothing 'cept maybe his head." Her smile faded then, perhaps because of her discomfort, perhaps because of her memories. "Man thought maybe he knew more than he did," she said pensively. "And, course maybe I believed he did, least for a while. Yes, sir, for a while after I first married him I thought maybe he knowed more than most. Back then he was coming and going on the rails so much I reckoned maybe he had learned a thing or two, something worth payin' attention to."

"On the railroad? Where?" Chuck asked. "Where'd he go?"

"Well, them lines came in from every direction right into the heart of Chattanooga. Must have been four or five companies running them trains. And Peter, well, he went down to CHEHAW more times than I can count," she said, dragging out the second syllable until it was forced to drop off her tongue. "CHEHAAAAAAW." She leaned back against the pillows that had been placed behind her, then rubbed her hands together, gently, and I noticed they, too, were swollen, her palms patchy with a rash. She tugged on her wedding ring, absently, before continuing. "Going down there to that place seemed like the only one thing Peter ever did do right."

"How come?"

Amelia rubbed her shoulder and straightened the front of her nightgown. She seemed to ache all over, but she kept talking. "Well, seems that place down there had them a school for Negroes that weren't far from the rail lines—a college there in Tuskegee where colored folks is allowed to go and get themselves a degree." She paused for a moment and helped Chuck with a plastic pearl that had shriveled and looked like an albino raisin. "I used to think on that a lot. Fact, I was gonna send my nephew, Perry Lee, to that there school," she continued, rubbing the pearl between her fingers to warm it and make the plastic expand. "Soon as I finished up paying for him to get out of jail, I was gonna send him to get hisself an education." And there was pride in her voice, pride in the thought, for a moment. "But it got to be too late. Boy got too old for school."

I looked at the box of beads, scared to ask why Perry Lee was in jail because she and Mama taught us not to stick our nose in business that didn't have anything to do with us. I was scared to ask the wrong question and scared not to ask because then she'd stop telling the story. "How come he went to jail?" I whispered.

"Nothing but the color of his skin," she answered without hesitation and took a sip from the Mason jar she kept filled with water on the bedside table. "Nobody saying that, but that's the truth of it."

Her words hung in the air and at first, I didn't believe her. She'd never said anything like that before, and I couldn't help but look at her—at her dark skin that shone with sweat and the two short salt-and-pepper-colored braids she rolled together at the back of her neck. Why would such a thing be true? And then I thought about Daddy saying, "The jails are full of Negroes," and I remembered he said most Negroes belonged in jail. Just few weeks earlier, he'd said more than seven hundred had been arrested in Georgia because they wanted their "civil rights," another term he spat out with derision. He'd said that our damn president Kennedy got them all stirred up. I didn't know what my father was talking about at the time, but I knew that if Amelia said her nephew was put in jail because of the color of his skin, she was telling the truth.

"But what'd Perry Lee do?" Chuck asked.

"Sheriff say Perry Lee done shot his gun at them Klan. Course I always knowed that ain't what happened, cause if he had, he would have hit 'em. Boy knew how to use a gun. He'd been shootin' coons for supper his whole life and had him a good aim. Now he sure enough may have got his gun out when them KKK come sniffin' around his mama's house, but he didn't shoot at nobody. He would've knowed better." She tossed the dried-up pearl back into the tin box and pulled the blanket more tightly over her lap. I looked down, feeling ashamed for having asked, as by then I'd heard at school about how the Klan hated Negroes and had lynching raids at night. I'd even heard a boy telling his friends that his daddy thought the Klan might have moved into New Jersey to put a stop to some Northern Jews but again, I didn't know what it all meant and had not thought that these things had anything to do with Amelia.

"Perry Lee's mama was my oldest sister, God rest her soul. Perry Lee weren't but about fifteen or sixteen, and maybe he should've knowed better than to even pick up that gun, if'n he did pick it up. But Klan worser than any rattlesnake. Klan got a mean streak worse than snake poison, and that ain't no lie."

"Mama says we can't say 'ain't,'" Chuck interrupted.

Amelia looked at him and her face changed with a slight frown, as if she were remembering how young he was or that maybe she'd been saying too much. "And she's right. Ain't ain't in the dictionary. But a body can't just be changing a lifetime of saying something so easy." She rolled the Mason jar between her hands, flinched when it rolled against the inside of her knuckles, then eased it between the numerous vials of pills on her bedside table, and picked up her small black Bible. Leaning back into her pillow, she let her hands fall into her lap, holding the Bible as Chuck shifted the snap beads into a pile between his legs. Her movements had taken a lot of effort, and I could see a shine on her forehead, sweat, maybe fever.

"Well, the sheriff put Perry Lee in jail," Amelia continued, looking at me and sighing. "And then I had to get some money from the bondsman to get him out. Long time ago. Lord, that was a long time ago, and I's still paying that man. Every week I send him four or five dollars. Figure I got a few more years before I get it all paid, if he don't add any more of what he calls 'interest,' that is. Perry Lee never did get to go to that school, but it don't matter none. Boy turned out just fine. Just fine." She sounded tired.

"What about that place, CHEHAW?" I asked, not wanting her to stop, but wanting to hear about something less sad.

She looked confused for a moment. "CHEHAW is down in Alabama. Why you want to know?"

"'Cause you said Peter—"

"Peter was riding the railroad. That would have been the Central Georgia Railroad that stopped at that station. I remember how I thought it was the strangest sounding name for a town. Course, I don't know now if it was the name of the town of if'n it stood for something else, but it don't matter. That's where colored folk got off. Some of them going to the flying school and some of them going to that college there that got started by Booker T. Washington."

"There's a flying school?" Chuck looked excited.

"Don't be getting no big ideas. It ain't no place for you. They be teaching colored men there to fly airplanes going to war."

She was tired and talkative at the same time. Still, I believed she was in bed only because her legs hurt.

"Did Peter know how to fly?" I asked, pushing her to go on.

"Lord, no. He was there for the railroad." She didn't say anything more, and I held up the string of plastic pearls I'd snapped together for her, put them back into the tin, and then reached for her books of green stamps to count how many pages were filled.

"Don't be getting into them stamps," she said, stopping me. "I ain't wanting to know how many I got 'cause I know it ain't much. I ain't saved nothing for a couple few weeks."

"Didn't Mama give you hers?"

"Not that I remember, child. She gives them to me when she don't forget. Now you gonna read me a chapter out of the Bible? Teach your ol' Mimi how to read some?"

Chuck snuggled closer to her to look over her shoulder at her holy pictures. She never let us hold those pictures, but always smiled when she pulled them from inside her soft, leather-covered Bible.

"Um hum. This one telling us about those green pastures where we be going when we cross over." She showed Chuck the brightly colored print of fair-skinned Jesus sitting with a newborn lamb on his lap with beautiful green hills covered in spring flowers behind him.

"When are we going there?" Chuck asked.

"When the Lord calls us, child. When it's our time."

Chuck cocked his head, clearly not sure of what she meant.

"When you cross over," I whispered, noticing the comfort those pictures gave Amelia, the peaceful expression around her mouth as her finger traced the colors. "When you die."

"Oh," Chuck said, without looking at me.

Amelia pulled forth a less-colorful frontal image of Jesus with a large halo around his head and his hand held as if blessing the viewer while staring straight ahead.

"Look how his eyes follow you around," Chuck said. "Same as those pictures in your room," he teased irreverently, flashing his eyes as he referred to the four portraits of my mother's ancestors we both agreed were frightening. "Creepy . . ."

"Ain't creepy, child. The Lord sees everything you do. He's watching you, watching out for you."

"My favorite is the picture at the wedding where he blessed the wine and bread to feed the multitudes."

"Ain't the way the story goes, but that wine would surely be sweet."

"Yuck."

"How do you know it's yuck?" I asked.

"Haven't you ever tasted it? Take a sip out of one of the bottles downstairs."

Amelia sat straight up. "Don't you tell me you been drinking your daddy's wine?"

Chuck cowered. "No, ma'am. I just took a sip."

"Don't you be taking no sips. Don't you put that bottle to your lips, never. You hear me? I seen enough drinking and carrying on for ten lives. And you best pray you ain't going in that direction. Child, I ever hear of you drinking I come out and take a switch to you so hard you won't be able to sit. You hear me?"

Chuck looked completely confused. "Yes, ma'am. I won't, Mimi."

"You promise me right here on the Bible. Put your hand on it and promise me."

She took Chuck's small hand and placed it under her own on top of the Bible. "I swear to the Lord I ain't gonna be no drinker. Never. Go on, say it after me."

Chuck muttered the words.

"Girl, you gonna say it, too. Ain't nothing stopping fine ladies from being drunks. Fall-down, mean, good-for-nothing drunks. Fact is, it seems like white women hides it better than colored, but they don't hide nothing inside their own houses and I seen inside plenty of white folks houses."

"Mimi, why are you getting mad?" I asked.

"I ain't mad at you, child, but I ain't letting you and Chuck turn out like some kind of no-account. And the fastest way to that is drinking."

"Who's a no-account?"

"Well, now," her voice dropped and she hesitated. "I don't rightly think you know any no-accounts like I'm talking about. Not yet, least-ways." She put the pictures in the back of the Bible. "But I can tell you, drinking comes before the fall."

"What's the fall?"

"Before you hit bottom, rock bottom. That's what."

Chuck and I both waited for her to explain. "Like Peter," she began, "Like that." Her voice dropped and she settled back into the pillows. "My daddy had to believe Peter was a good man before he told me to marry him," she continued, wistfully, then shook her head. "Peter was too old for me," she said with firmness. "It was clear soon as I looked at him, but my daddy said he'd be a good husband."

"Wasn't your daddy right?" Chuck asked.

"No," I whispered, surprised he'd asked.

Amelia looked at him as if deciding whether he was old enough for her story. She ran her fingers over the cover of her Bible and looked up to the ceiling like she was about to pray. I held my breath.

"Child, a good husband looks after his family. A good husband puts food on the table and comes home at night. That's what you're gonna do someday. You gonna work and make some woman proud. Now, Peter, well the man had some habits, like that drinking, too strong for me to change. He was plain too set in his ways."

"Where'd you meet him?" Chuck asked.

"Don't rightly remember meeting him other than my daddy introducing him one day at suppertime."

"Your daddy brought him home?"

Amelia laughed slightly. "Like a stray dog. But my daddy was too old hisself to know better. Lord, he was getting on to nearly seventy

years old when I was barely making it to fourteen. Now you remember, I was the youngest of all them children, thirteen of them. Can
you imagine such a thing? And, well, Daddy was doing his best."

"What about your mama?"

"Poor woman plain gave out when I was born. Had enough of all
that birthing. She passed on before I even opened my eyes. Daddy says
the midwife told him it was better that way—kept whatever it was that
sucked out her life from getting in me through my eyes. Course I don't
know about that. Seems like a curse not having no mama."

My breath seemed stuck in my throat. Amelia had never told us
this story. I inched forward, not knowing what to ask, or if I should ask
anything.

"You didn't have a mama?" Chuck asked incredulously.

Amelia patted his hand. "Long time ago now, child. Not something
I even think about much anymore, but seems like things might have
been different if I'd had one. Still, the Lord had his plans for me, so I
ain't gonna complain."

"What happened? Where were your brothers and sisters? Did they
take care of you?"

"Most of them were near about growed and gone by the time I
came along. I was what they called a change-of-life baby."

"Huh?"

She looked at both of us, again deciding what to tell us. Her glasses
were smudged with fingerprints. "Well, never you mind about that. Just
means my mama was getting old, but all in all, I guess my daddy did
his best. Sent me to school until the second grade, even though I don't
remember learning nothing much 'cept how to sit still, and then after
that I worked them fields for a while until he found Peter for me, and
I know my daddy believed he was doing right."

Amelia's eyes filled with tears, but she didn't let them fall. I wanted
to hear about the romance, how they fell in love, how she was crying
because she missed him.

"Peter got himself fancied up and made Daddy believe . . . well, Daddy needed some money real bad by then and . . . oh, Lord, there ain't no good in telling this story. You children don't need to know all that. I's trying to tell you about the drink," she inhaled deeply and spread her hands flat in front of her.

"Now, Peter was a good twenty years older than me and I couldn't do nothing about him, but I knows what drink can do—whiskey, wine, bootleg, mash, whatever kind you be thinking of, it all do the same— makes a man mean and a woman cheap. And there ain't nothing I won't do to keep you children away from it."

"But Mama and Daddy drink."

"I know that, child, but I want you to promise right now that you won't. I want you to pray and I'll pray for you. Ain't nothing but the devil in a bottle." She picked up the Bible and held out. "I wants you both to swear right here and now on this Bible you won't be drinking no devil water."

I didn't like swearing on the Bible. The sisters at school said you couldn't go back on whatever you swore to on the Bible. "How come, Mimi?"

"You ain't figured it out yet, girl? I knows you know it get dark and mean inside this house."

I nodded. Chuck picked at the threads on the edge of the blanket.

Amelia set the Bible on my lap and I put my hand over the inlaid gold cross. "You swear on this here Bible that long as you live you ain't gonna be drinking that devil water. You ain't gonna set yourself up with no glass of wine and no martini or old fashioned. No nothing. You just plain ain't gonna drink that foolishness."

"I promise," I said, meaning it, but really wanting to move away from these thoughts.

She put Chuck's hand on the Bible. "You promise too, boy."

"But I already did. You already made me."

"Alright, then."

We all three sat quietly. Amelia took off her glasses and wiped the lenses on the edge of the spread.

"But, Mimi," Chuck said, "where are your brothers and sisters?"

"I don't know, child. Last time I went home, I heard tell one of my sisters is over there in Philadelphia where that Liberty Bell is, but nobody knew what her last name is now. She been married two or three times, I guess. I'd ask your mama to help me find her, but it ain't no use."

"But what about the rest of them?" I asked.

"Well, my family didn't come from Chattanooga. I only moved there once Peter and I was married, 'cause that where the railroad lines—the Great Southern and the Cincinnati and what all—all cross together. Seems like everybody I knowed in that town worked on them lines. Peter, well he got to see a big piece of the world that way. Like I told you, he went on out to that CHEHAW in that direction. Got to see that there school for coloreds and even got himself treated by some fine doctors there. That was 'long about the year nineteen thirty-seven, and fact is, for a while I thought he'd be cured of that bad blood he had. Said he got some of them pink pills they be givin' out to the men in Macon, and that they gonna give him some insurance if he take them. Man said he was gonna get himself some insurance. But I don't guess he did what they told him, or maybe . . . oh, Lord knows. I just knows I sure never saw no insurance. But I knows the train line took him over there couple times a year and he told me how them men in those parts were getting some treatment. Said that's what got rid of his bad blood. And he weren't sick none, didn't have him them sores none, so I figured . . . well, I don't know what all I figured, but that train line took him to Ohio and on up into Pennsylvania and he always had some story to tell. Some of them stories were good ones, good ones like letting me know about that there school for coloreds. I started saving every penny I could save, 'cause I figured Perry Lee could get hisself an education going to that school, make something of hisself. And, well," her voice changed, "well, never no mind that right now, I's trying to tell you about Peter."

"Before the fall?" Chuck asked, noticing her confusion, or perhaps his own. Neither one of us knew what she was talking about, except that Peter drank a lot and worked on the railroad.

"That's right. Before the fall. Man always did drink. He was drinking when he and my daddy agreed to us getting married. And he was drinking when the minister pronounced us. He near about falling down drunk when Sylvester got born and then he was out cold most of the time that boy was alive. Sobered up some when Sylvester crossed over, but you know, it was too late by then."

"What do you mean?"

She looked at Chuck, pushed his hair back from his forehead, then let her hand drop into her lap. "Well, near as I can explain it," she said gently, her voice soft, "when you lose a child, nothing that comes after matters much. That was the fall." She inhaled deeply before continuing. "And Peter sure didn't matter much to me after that."

"Where is he?"

"Can't hardly guess no more." She looked at her wedding ring. "The Lord brought us together and we been married going on fifty years now and I don't know his whereabouts. Could be dead. Should be. He was more than seventy when your daddy sent him back on down the line and I ain't seen him since."

"Don't you want to?"

"No. Only thing I want is knowing he gone."

Chuck climbed off the bed. "Mama says we can't stay up here long because you'll get tired."

"Um hum."

"You think we can go see that school one day?" he asked.

"Sure you can, child. Sure you can."

I took Mimi's Bible and put it on her bedside table. She grabbed my hand. "Thank you, child. You're good to your old Mimi."

But I didn't feel like I'd been good to her. I didn't feel like any of what she'd told us was good.

When I went back downstairs I asked my mother, who was trying a new recipe, if she had some green stamps we could give Amelia the next day. "Oh, they're just over there in the drawer. Didn't I give them to her?" As I pulled them out of the drawer, I asked her about the train lines in Chattanooga.

"Well, there are several. But they're mostly freight lines and mostly coloreds working on them, but they keep the city rich. And now with the Chattanooga Choo Choo, they make the city famous, too."

I counted twelve pages of stamps and wondered why she'd forgotten to give them to Amelia, but as she seemed preoccupied and happy to talk, I asked her if she knew Amelia was paying somebody to keep her nephew out of jail.

"She's been doing that as long as I've known her. Every week she mails that man money. I told her once that she probably didn't need to anymore, but she's scared they will put Perry Lee back in jail if she stops." She laughed slightly. "That sheriff has probably made a fortune from the coloreds. They just don't have any sense."

And her words stopped me cold. I didn't dare ask anything else. I'd never heard her talk like my father.

Palm Sunday

THE STEEP STEPS up to Amelia's third-floor room were without carpet. Wood boards with traces of worn paint gave a blue hue to the narrow stairwell that echoed with the slightest footstep. I'd learned to tiptoe when I climbed the stairs to see her, minimizing any noise that would draw attention from my parents, and allowing me to surprise Amelia by popping my head straight up by her rug. But that Sunday—Palm Sunday—I ran up without a care, making noise like thunder with the hard soles of my scuffed patent-leather shoes, and stumbled close to the top as I held the long leaves of the branch of palm that had been given to us at the end of Mass.

"I got an extra one for you, Mimi," I called out happily, ignoring the bash I'd taken against my shin and noting the dimness of the room in stark contrast to the brightness of the rest of the house—as if spring had not reached through these high windows but had stopped at the bottom of the stairs.

Amelia was sleeping. The curtains were pulled nearly shut, allowing only a tiny shaft of light marred by dust particles to reach the edge of her bed.

"Mimi," I whispered, inching between the overstuffed boxes and her rumpled spread to draw back the fading material. The edge of a palm leaf felt sharp against my hand. "Mimi," I whispered again as I opened the window and let in the glorious spring morning.

"I heard you, child," she answered as the first chirp of a multitude of birds gently pierced the gloominess of the room and she pushed her glasses to the bridge of her nose while pulling the covers up to her neck. "I heard you."

"Look!" I held the two palms out to her. I gave her both, although one was for me. There was such strong delight in having her to myself I would have given her anything, and it was this warm abandon that allowed me to quickly sit on the side of the bed and use my toes to push my shoes off. The palm leaves curled toward their middles, but only the slightly sharp edges gave me pause. "This one is about as tall as me," I said proudly, taking the yellow-colored leaf and waving it in the air above her face.

"Sure 'nough," she agreed, smiling and catching hold without expressing irritation. "These are good palms, good ones. I'll show you how to weave them, make a bookmark for the Bible out of them. Just like we did last year. You remember that, child?"

"I still have it, Mimi."

"Good. That's good. Lord wants us to remember how He faced what was coming." She pushed herself up against her pillows, dragging the covers higher.

"How come you're still sleeping?"

"Just need my rest. You want to hand me that water? I'll get up by and by, but it feels good to stay put. Feels real good."

I leaned across her feet and grabbed hold of the half-full Mason jar on her side table. "You want some fresh water?" I stood. "I'll get you some."

I carried the jar to her bathroom and dumped the old water down the sink, then refilled it and brought it back to her.

"Bless you, child. I love cool water."

"I know," I said, proud to have done something for her as I crossed my legs under my slip, which made me realize I'd only have a few minutes before I'd have to change my clothes. Chuck was already changing his, and I enviously thought he was probably smarter than me as now he'd be able to visit Amelia longer. "Chuck got a whole handful of palms," I whispered with self-pity.

"Did he now?"

"And Lizzy already cut hers up so she can make whistles out of them."

"Um hum. But I don't see how whistles are gonna remind her of the Lord."

"I don't know," I shrugged, feeling singled out, special, to be having this conversation. "And, well," I sputtered, trying to find the best way to continue, "Michael didn't want to keep his and Father McNamara frowned kinda mean at him, and then Norma gave hers to Lizzy."

"So I guess putting all that together means Chuck's bringing his up here and we're gonna make us a few bookmarks."

"Yep." I turned my face away, pretending to listen to the birds as I hoped he wouldn't come too soon.

Amelia watched me, curved one of the leaves around her hand, and tested its flexibility. "These sure are two fine palm leaves," she said, obviously trying to soothe things, trying to make me feel happy again. "Don't be sulking on this day. This day is about facing what's to come and finding strength to carry on."

Something about her voice caught my attention. "What do you mean? They used palms to wave at Jesus when he rode the donkey into Jerusalem. That's all." I took the second one from her lap.

"Uh huh, but didn't Jesus know what was gonna happen? Didn't He know He only had a week left to be in this world? And He was accepting that. He was going on, riding that donkey even though He knowed what was to come."

I twisted the palm leaf and ran my finger along the sharp edge of it.

"That's what I always think about on this day. Accepting what's to come. Accepting what is."

"What do you mean?" I echoed.

"Well, I've been thinking about it. Sitting up in this bed trying to get my rest, falling asleep in the middle of one thought and waking up in the middle of another. I've been thinking about it. Years ago, we had us a preacher told us about how Palm Sunday had a whole lot of sadness to it, but that it was like the calm before the storm, like when you know a storm is coming and you get yourself ready."

"I thought Jesus did that back in . . . when he . . ."

"Could be. But it could be that when He was riding that donkey He was thinking, 'I'm heading right toward it now so I best let this animal carry me and not do nothing, not try and change it or keep up the good fight, or nothing. Just be carried.'"

"That's not—"

"Let me finish, child. Let me finish. I been up here thinking on things, on you and Chuck, and, well, let me finish."

"Why are you thinking about us?"

"Just thinking. Just thinking how you keep quiet, keeping to yourself, all the while you be hoping Lizzy and Norma gonna take some kind of notice of you. And then how you knows them boys ain't gonna be playing with you 'cause they's boys, 'cepting you still keep hoping least Chuck will . . . well, you know what I'm talking about, child?"

"I guess."

"You knows. I knows it, too, and I'm telling you this is Palm Sunday and that's what you gots to be learning today. You got to learn to be accepting what they be calling the natural order of things. You heard that expression. Your daddy uses it sometime when he talking about colored folks working for white folks, but that ain't what I'm talking about."

Her words were hard to follow, hard to take in, hard to react to without my stomach twisting into a knot and my hands sliding along the palm's edge.

"I's talking about you being birthed into this family. You got yourself two sisters and two brothers. That's the natural order for you. And that's what it's gonna be. Ain't no use trying to do nothing about it. Them girls are glued together 'cause they got borned together and them boys is brothers and that's a bond that can't be pushed or pulled by nobody 'cept them. So, where does that leave you?" She inhaled and I couldn't help but think she was angry with me and I didn't know why. "Well, it means the Lord got something else in mind for you. I don't know what. And truth be told, maybe you won't never know what, but what you got here today is a way to accept it and go on about your business. Go on knowing. Knowing. Leastways, you got that. You got that knowing that this is the way it is meant to be. It's the natural order of things. The way God wanted it to be. You keep on getting your feelings all bunched up and aching, when this ain't nothing you can change or do nothing about. Them girls ain't thinking about you. They ain't thinking about nothing 'cept each other. They ain't thinking you even part of things. And that may be harsh, but that, well, that's just where you got birthed."

My stomach hurt so bad that tears formed, and I kept trying to hear the birds, not wanting to hear her voice. "Mimi, how come you're getting mad at me?"

Her hands dropped to her sides leaving the palm lying on her stomach, and after a moment she leaned forward and took my hand in hers. Awkward, not like when she held it as she pulled me along the platform at the train station or when she pulled me forward to meet Aunt Ruth. It felt awkward because there was no movement, just the warmth of her broad, brown hand with callused palms cradling my much smaller, white, smooth hand.

"I ain't mad," she said softly. "I's just thinking on things. Just trying to do what the Lord wants me to do and it seems to me He wants me to tell you what I been seeing. And I been seeing since the day you was born that He got something else in mind for you than being somebody's sister." She squeezed my fingers. "I saw it clearly when Chuck got born. Way that evened it out. Two girls, two boys, and you in the middle. Now you can be trying to be a sister to all of them you whole life, but it ain't meant to be. Not the way Norma and Elizabeth are sisters. And not the way Chuck and Michael are brothers. No, child, the Lord got something else in mind for you and sooner you accept that, the better off you will be."

I knew she was right, but I didn't want to believe it. "Then how come I'm in this family?" I asked, furious at the suggestion. "How come?"

She shook her head. "Lord knows," she answered, sounding more like herself. "Lord knows. But we all got to be accepting, and we got to accept what is coming."

"What's coming?"

"I don't know, child. I don't know." A breeze blew the curtain and a chill reminded me that spring was still young. "Like I say, only the Lord knows what is to come," she said. "But you got this palm at church today, so you let it remind you of what we been talking about—accepting what you knows is the truth, same as Jesus accepted what was gonna come. You let it . . ."

"Mimi! Mimi!" Chuck called as his feet pounded against the wood stairs like thunder until he breathlessly stood before us. "Let's make some book markers. Mama says I can give one to my teacher tomorrow. Here, I brought you up these lilacs. Mama said you aren't feeling well." He reached the top of the stairs carrying a huge bouquet of blossoming purple lilacs cut from the hedge in the backyard. The scent filled the air and the tiny drops of water on their leaves sparkled with the freshness he'd brought to the room.

"That's my boy, my boy," Amelia whispered, her eyes filling with silent tears and unspoken joy. She held my hand for another moment, then let go to receive Chuck's gift.

April 18, 1964

FOR WEEKS, AMELIA lay on her back propped up with pillows in her queen-sized bed. The rumpled space around her was piled high with the pastimes of a person with a prolonged illness—half-finished stitched pillowcases, tin cans full of plastic snap-beads, an open Bible, and boxes of ribbon candy and fading photographs of long-dead relatives. I ran my finger along the scalloped edges of the one photo—a relic of her dark-eyed, sweet-smiling son, Sylvester.

"He was a good-looking boy. Good looking and . . ." Amelia's proud words were always the same and uttered with passion equal to the first time she'd showed me that photo. "He would have growed to be tall, tall like Peter but a good man. . . ."

Amelia's room had always been cluttered, but after so many weeks of being sick, it was dirty, and it lacked comfort. The unpacked wardrobe boxes containing Sylvester's clothing and the few dresses she had worn as a young woman were still stacked by the wall at the foot of the bed—torn at the corners, sagging in the middle, and covered with crayon drawings or scribbles where my brothers and sisters had decided to decorate years ago without her permission. The square of dark-brown carpet that spanned between the bed and rocking chair still provided some cohesion to the room, but it was filthy, heavily sprinkled with the bits and pieces of the many days that had passed since she'd become sick. And there was a tray with an untouched cup of coffee and a soggy piece of buttered toast balanced precariously on the marble-topped dresser next to her. I wondered when Mama had brought it for her.

"You see how fine his hair was? That child was gonna be something."

I glanced over at the large wood-cased television topped with tall antenna ears and layered with so much dust that fingerprints on the screen merged with static. Fred MacMurray was talking, calmly as always, wearing a perfectly ironed shirt and tie. The room behind him was without a hint of clutter. I didn't know what episode of *My Three Sons* it was, but was glad someone had pushed the television at an angle so Amelia could watch it from her bed.

"You watching this?" I asked, interrupting her, old enough to be irritated by the repetition of her thoughts and the uncomfortable dusting of jealousy they provoked, while still too young to understand how closely I should have been listening, how carefully I should have been savoring the preciousness of her memories.

"No, child, I ain't watching that." She held her hand out for me to return the photograph, then smiled gently at her son's face before slipping it back between the pages of her Bible. I turned toward the television.

In February, we had seen Ed Sullivan introduce the Beatles. Chuck and I had been sitting next to Amelia making jokes about Ringo Starr's face being distorted with swerving lines from a thumbprint anchoring him between the cymbals of his drum set.

"Those boys are gonna make a lot of money. See how them girls be acting? Yes, sir, they gonna make a lot of money. Like Elvis. Now, go get you a rag and wipe those fingerprints off the screen," Amelia instructed as she'd watched with the same excitement we all had.

Her illness then was a welcome break in our routines. We could remove ourselves from the rest of the house and sit up on her bed and watch television or work on our homework while eating snacks. But that was back when she still had a little energy, when I assumed it was her swollen legs keeping her off her feet, and that it wouldn't take much time before she was back down in the kitchen. That was back before taking dinners up to her on a tray, waiting, then bringing the dirty dishes back down to be washed was not a daily task. It was before I was given the job of vacuuming and cleaning for my mother's parties, and before sitting in the kitchen and chopping vegetables became a required part of Saturdays. That was before a few months had passed and she was still in bed, and *The Ed Sullivan Show* had become a marker for the changing weeks. I noticed with a twinge of guilt that the fingerprints were still on the television screen, but by then, her sickness had become a chore, and I was too irritated to want to clean it for her.

The rocking chair still faced her bed, the seat stacked with the same towels and sheets she'd washed just after Christmas, before she'd had her first "spell." That's what Mama called it. Now the linen had been sat upon and pushed down in the middle like an old pillow, but Amelia no longer cared. Nor did she care that her bed was made with someone else's laundered goods, or that her food was brought at odd times. And she couldn't always remember who it was that made the bed, or who brought her food. She couldn't remember that my mother sat with her and listened to her tell stories of Sylvester, or that Chuck and I had grown tired of keeping her company.

The banisters to the stairwell that led down to the second floor were draped with her maid's uniform, thick stockings, and a worn gray sweater. Amelia hadn't been down the steps since a cold morning in February. Now it was April 18, 1964. I was eleven years old.

Lent and Easter had passed and it was warm outside. It was Saturday, the kind of day that calls for children to be running or riding their bikes—the kind of day that gives glory to the idea of spring and makes one feel like rejoicing for no particular reason. Mama said it was my turn to stay home with Amelia. She and Daddy were going grocery shopping, and the rest, my brothers and sisters, were going to play in the neighborhood. I didn't think it was fair and said so, then waited until the house was quiet before begrudgingly making lemonade from frozen concentrate in a can and taking it upstairs with me to give to Amelia.

The lemonade was pink and full of pulp. Amelia motioned for me to put it on the bedside table while she tried to push herself into a more upright position against her pillows. I held it instead, feeling it cold against my fingers, and waited, watching the dust particles in the sunbeam streaming through her window, and wondered if I'd be able to ride my bike later that afternoon.

"Put it down, child," she whispered, her voice low and hoarse.

Pill bottles crowded most of the table but were easily inched aside by the base of the glass. Amelia had hardly moved any farther up on her pillow. She looked uncomfortable and her color was strange, a grayish-brown like dried tree bark. Mama would have leaned over her and helped her, pushed pillows behind her and pulled her up under her arms. I didn't think I should, unless she asked.

She started talking, quietly, muttering to the Lord about lambs. It was as if I wasn't there and I started feeling the sadness that had threatened to overwhelm me for the past several days. It was sadness so deep that I had buried it, distanced myself from it with rebellion and irritation. But there, watching Amelia unable to sit up, there was no way to turn from it. No way to hide or understand. I was too young.

I sat in the rocking chair and stared at her lips moving in prayer and remembered that a few days earlier she had told me the Lord didn't mind that she didn't always know who I was, or my brothers and sisters, who brought her things like the palms that stuck out of the bottle by her bed. She'd said as long as she remembered her Sylvester, and that the Lord knew she was counting on seeing her boy again, she didn't believe it really mattered much if she forgot others. She said she hoped I didn't mind—it wasn't nothing to do with me.

But she was wrong, and I didn't know how she could say such a thing. It was a lot to do with me, Chuck, and all of us. But I didn't know what. I only knew I couldn't imagine that Amelia wouldn't remember who I was and I couldn't let Chuck know what she'd said. I had to forget that she'd said such a thing. I had to believe she didn't mean it.

She was, I think, trying to be kind in explaining, as she knew she'd started rambling in her conversations and was worried about what she might say. I didn't know how unclear her thoughts had become, but I remembered we looked away from each other, and we'd looked around her room, absorbing whatever we could to make us feel better. It was then that I realized that perhaps we really weren't a part of her the same way she was a part of us.

Her room was her sanctuary. Her privacy. It was where she held her memories clear. In each corner and in each box, there was an inventory of memories that helped her to recall vivid moments of her past. A rope belt her father had worn and the cracked hand mirror that belonged to a mother she'd never known. A dented flask left behind by her husband. Her son's schoolbooks, faded socks, and play clothes. She could dream about a closet where one day she would lovingly store all the quilt materials folded in her boxes and the memories using the cloth-covered hangers she'd made with her church group. And in that thought was the realization that her boxes held nothing from us. Nothing from Chuck and me, my sisters, or Michael. Nothing from my mother or father. We had merely scribbled on the outside of the boxes. Nothing she'd kept sacred had anything to do with her six years of living in that room with our family.

Maybe if she had something of ours in the boxes, I wouldn't feel afraid she'd forget who we were. It was a stretch, a grasp at straws, but it gave me a newfound determination that washed over me with visions of knitting and sewing projects. I'd put something in the top box. Chuck could make her a clay bowl or find the oven mitt he wove for her the summer before. Norma and Elizabeth could make paintings and Michael could carve his name into some birch bark. I could fix this problem. I could make sure Amelia had memories of us in her boxes. I could surprise her with these new treasures, and then she wouldn't forget who we were.

I watched as she inhaled with difficulty, and I tried to rationalize that she was going to get better. Huffing and puffing was normal for her. And besides, Amelia always said that it was the pain in her bones that caused her to curse the devil, the swelling in her ankles and knees, the stiffness in her fingers. Nothing seemed to help that, she'd said. Huffing and puffing was second nature.

She stopped praying and pushed herself into a slightly better sitting position, ignoring that her nightgown, caught behind her, pulled tightly at her neck. I could see it took a lot of energy to just move those few inches. As I continued to daydream about presents for her boxes, she said her heart drummed in her head.

"Let me catch my breath," she whispered and sank back down into the mattress. She then stretched her arm to her side toward her Bible, and having touched it, she moved her fingertips farther over the leather to feel the curled edges of the photographs—her Sylvester. Her glasses fogged. She managed to lift her head just high enough to look over her covers.

"Sugar?" she whispered.

I knew Amelia wasn't talking to me and was scared to look at her. Instead, I thought about making a knitted blanket, about using the colors she loved—the light-pink in the quilt she'd hemmed and the greens in the threads that she'd embroidered on her pillow cases—and I started feeling happy, happy that I could do something for her.

"Sugar pie?"

❖

The little girl looked familiar and the endearment felt comfortable, but the girl didn't hear her and Amelia decided she might be dreaming. She lay back and tried to relax. She wanted to pull her nightgown away from her neck, but couldn't lift her hands. She focused on the moment, on the feeling of the sheet covering her feet, and decided if she could just control her breathing maybe the weight would lift from her chest.

The child was quiet. Amelia stared at the slant of the ceiling and felt a breeze from the half-open window. It was her favorite season, the most beautiful time of the year. Nice things always happened to her in the spring. Things she could count on. Things that had changed her. She knew this from years of experience, years of trusting the Lord to bring good things with good weather. Even when she was a child and washing her one dress every day, she knew she could count on the spring to help her. After all, the touch of warmth that arrived in March helped the thin cotton fabric dry quickly, keeping it from clinging cold in the mornings, protecting her from shivers and hungry stares. And spring brought the scent of fresh vegetables, of tomatoes that would grow and swell, pumpkins that spread tendrils, and bean vines with blossoms. There was always such promise. Promise like when her boy was born. Her Sylvester. That tiny baby who she'd been blessed with and kept holy for his twelve little years. And they were little. Too-short years that were tightly wound up in the confines of the houses she worked in or in the dark rooms she shared with his father, the man that she wanted to forgive. She prayed to God to forgive him but couldn't make her bones stop aching long enough to believe she'd forgiven him. But it was a fine April day that brought Sylvester, a day just like today, and she couldn't help but be filled with her love for him as she lay there on the bed trying to catch her breath.

"Sugar," she whispered through her fingers inside her Bible, touching the edge of his photo, remembering every detail of the way he'd looked, his smooth brown skin and giant round eyes. And the tears welled beneath her glasses, and as they dripped back over her temples and into her hair, she was comforted by them, and by the gallons more she had wept.

"Sugar . . ."

She prayed the lessons she'd learned at church were correct—that she'd meet him once again. But she wasn't ready to cross over yet, even though her bones ached so bad she didn't think she'd ever bend her knees or comb her hair again. Even though her breath seemed stuck in the base of her neck and her simple plans to look at the Bible were failing.

"Sugar?" she whispered yet again, and this time she heard the little white child answering as if from another room.

"Mimi? What medicine do you want, Mimi? What medicine should I give you?"

"Sugar . . ."

The table next to the bed she knew was covered with bottles of tablets and syrups. No one had ever said what was making her sick. No one had to. She'd seen it in her Sylvester. In her baby. Heard it talked about. It was bad blood, plain and simple. And maybe she'd been born with it, or got it from Peter. And maybe the church ladies were right when they said it was a sign of ungodliness, her ungodliness, her bad temper or inability to forgive; maybe it was the Lord's punishment. But there was nothing ungodly about her child. And she didn't care one bit what anyone whispered, she knew he was in heaven. She knew the Lord would not punish so pure a child. And her minister had said he was that. Lamb of God.

Her chest lightened. Thank you, Lord. Whichever medicine would take the pain out of her fingers and toes or would let her breathe a little easier, she'd take it now. She tried to give direction to the child sitting in her rocking chair. "Sugar?"

"You want some more lemonade?" the child asked.

A little black dog came, stood on its back legs and sniffed her hand. The little girl picked it up and put it on the bed by her feet. "Do you want some medicine?"

The question tired her. Suddenly, a wave of tiredness washed over her and she wanted to tell the child to sit still and hold her hand, but she was too exhausted to find the words. She tried to reach for her but her fingers felt heavier than her heart and it seemed strange she didn't know who the child was. A white child. It seemed like she should know the child, but then it didn't seem all that *important.*

A hornet hit against the window screen and the little dog whimpered. Amelia remembered other hornets hitting screens in other places where it was so much warmer and frogs sang throughout the day. Her baby loved the frogs. He'd been so happy. He didn't know or maybe didn't want to know any of the badness his daddy brought into the house. He had snuggled in her arms, safe. Safe until he was too big to hold. But she could remember the feel of her hand gently touching his cheeks, and the look in his eyes as they began to cloud as she knew hers were now clouding.

Such a beautiful little boy that she'd made. Her throat tightened with her love. Had it been so long ago?

Mercifully, she then felt her baby heavy on her breast as if he were there, and thanking the Lord, Amelia tried to lift her hand to hold his head. Her baby's warmth spread through her heart and she sighed with utter happiness as the white girl's dog inched forward and pushed a wet nose under her hand. She couldn't wipe away her tears or clear the fog from her glasses.

"Sugar?" she tried again to whisper to the white child, wanting to show her the baby she'd given birth to, but there was no sound. The white girl had turned to look at the medicine bottles. Amelia's eyes filled with fog, like the clouds of heaven, and she drifted away with her beautiful brown baby on her chest.

❖

I picked up the glass of lemonade and turned back toward the bed, wondering if I should tell her about my idea to make her a blanket or keep it a surprise.

"You want me to hold the glass while you take a sip?" I asked, steadily growing happier, realizing I could sit with her for hours while knitting. "Which medicine do you want?"

Her eyes were open and she stared at the ceiling. The dog whimpered.

"Which medicine do you want? Which medicine . . . "

She didn't answer. I touched her hand, warm but unmoving.

I ran down the stairs to the phone in my parents' room and called

Mary M. Barrow

my sisters, my hand shaking when I had to call twice, amazed they wouldn't believe me that something was wrong until I screamed, "Just come home!"

And then I went back upstairs. There was nothing to say or do. It was quiet. So quiet. I sat on the end of the bed and pulled the dog onto my lap. Amelia's eyes were open. Her glasses were still on her nose. Her chest didn't rise or fall, her hand lay by her side and the covers were pulled up to just above her waist. There was nothing to say or do.

Last Moments

AMELIA WAS LAID out for viewing in the one-room Yardley Baptist Church during the evening before her funeral. Chuck sat in the front pew with Michael, his eyes dry but wide as the mothers of neighborhood children paid their respects, not to Amelia, but to my mother. I don't remember if my father was there. I don't remember any other fathers attending the viewing, although some did attend the funeral—Bob's father, Suzy's, and Kathy's. But the viewing was different. It was quiet, subdued.

There was no organ to play softly nor incense to burn silently, but two candles on the small altar reflected on the rough wooden floor, flickering over knolls and stretching flat beneath the bridge-like platform that held the casket. Amelia's friends—Aunt Lottie, Miss Ruthie, and Miss Josephine—stood like sentinels on either side. I was glad to see them. As Aunt Lottie leaned heavily on her cane, her hands gloved and her sweater hanging down from her shoulders too long over her wrists, I remembered that Amelia once said time shrank us down, and that she believed it was to make sure there was room for everyone in heaven.

Have you already gone to heaven?

I wasn't sure Amelia had really left. I understood the permanence of death, but it didn't feel like she was gone—it didn't feel like she wouldn't be in her room, or that she wouldn't be able to explain to me why her friends didn't wear their hats to the viewing, or why so few men came to see her that one last time, why men didn't sit quietly with the women. She was there, in her open coffin, in front of us. Her hair was combed neatly and held close to her head in a net. Her eyes were closed. Her large breasts were tightly corseted in deference to the size of the coffin. Her plump, round face was strangely hollow, and her skin was an ashen brown, no longer reminding me of newly baked bread, but like a creek rock dried in the sun.

I didn't like looking at her, but couldn't look away.

Her hands were crossed on top of her chest, her wedding ring finally loose on the withered skin where she'd tugged at it without thought. Her nails were still a color lighter than her palms.

It was hard to draw air into my lungs.

Her face was shrunken without her thick-rimmed glasses and her shoulders were without power. It was odd and I didn't like it. I didn't like how her breasts had been girdled or the way her dress was buttoned so close around her neck the fat beneath her chin spilled over it. I wanted to be able to say she looked calm or at peace, expressions I heard the nuns at school use when speaking of the dead, but I thought she simply looked still, smooth, cold, without texture. I didn't like looking at her. It hurt. The pain seared my tears before they could drip down my cheeks. I could only look away.

The walls of the church were painted blue and the windows didn't have vibrant stained glass that mesmerized me in the large church my family attended, but it felt familiar—it smelled like Amelia, like the witch hazel she rubbed on her swollen joints and that she put in her shoes to keep them dry. And I was glad to see women with her same color of skin and the same faded, floral dresses so thin their slips showed underneath, lopsided where they were pulled by the heavy sweaters worn on top. *Mimi, are you really gone?*

Mama, wearing white gloves she'd not worn for years and a fitted, long-sleeved dress belted at her waist, glanced over at Chuck, then glanced again at Amelia. She pushed her newly permed hair back from her forehead and whispered to Suzy's mother, turning as she did to keep watch on Chuck. But Chuck didn't move. When Michael left to roam by the canal behind the church with Lizzy and Norma, I slid next to Chuck and let my shoulder rub against his arm. Still, he didn't move. Clearly, everything in him had stopped, and maybe, unlike me, he didn't have the buffer of not really believing she was gone. Chuck looked like he needed someone to shake him. Chuck looked like he, too, had left.

Mama must have seen it, too. She whispered again to Suzy's mother who agreed to take Michael and my sisters for ice cream, then home. Mama then told Chuck and me to stay. I didn't dare leave Chuck's side and waited with worry as my mother stood at the church door speaking softly to the pastor, Reverend Cook, who would deliver the eulogy.

Chuck and I stared straight ahead as the church emptied and the night shadows flickered behind the two thick, round candles on the altar. We sat quietly. Miss Ruth came over and told us she was taking Aunt Lottie home, then she and Miss Josephine would be back to stay the night with Amelia. I hadn't thought about Amelia being alone during the night. I hadn't thought about how lonely it would be to sleep in an empty church with strange noises and a darkness deepened by the arched ceilings and empty pews. "Shouldn't we stay, too?" I asked.

"No, child. This be something her kinfolk do, and I believes she'd be wanting us to be thinking on her as such."

"But . . ."

She patted my shoulder and walked away. Chuck hadn't spoken. I turned in the pew, my legs slipping easily over the smooth wood surface, and watched her walk down the aisle. *Her kinfolk?* It made no sense, but the child in me accepted it and turned back toward her casket.

The voices around us faded as more and more people left and went home. I rubbed Chuck's shoulder and tried to give him a Smith Brothers cough drop, always his favorite, but he didn't respond. Nothing. It made me mad. It made me think he wasn't being fair. After all, he wasn't the only one who had lost Mimi, he wasn't the only one grieving. But deep down, I knew it was different for him. I knew Amelia had been his anchor in this world and that he'd been let go, that he was drifting, not knowing that somehow she was still there. And I didn't know how to catch him and tell him she hadn't completely left without sounding like I was lying.

Finally, the last visitors, a solemn group of older black men that included Mr. Thomas, who still drove his taxi, and Mr. Tom, who brought the bread each week came towards the altar. One by one, they filed past her, their right hands gliding affectionately along the shiny surface of the side of the casket as they muttered some private farewell. Together they then nodded toward Chuck and me, then walked back down the aisle, their shoes soft on the wooden floor, their heads hatless, and their shoulders hunched forward. They nodded toward my mother. Mr. Tom took her hand and said something about Amelia being with the Lord and that he was sorry for the loss they all felt. Mama nodded. Then all three men went out the front door, and Mama finally came to sit next to Chuck and me.

"I brought some pictures," Mama whispered to Chuck. "You can put them under her pillow."

Her words were like a small jolt of electricity, enough to shake me, but only for a moment. Chuck didn't answer, but his eyes moved slowly away from the coffin toward Mama's lap. He watched without expression as she took some square, ruffle-edged Kodak photos out of her handbag. I watched, too, surprised that Mama had actually thought of a way to address the very thing that had worried me most, that Amelia would forget us. Yet there in her lap, in black and white, was Chuck and me with Amelia at the beach on Block Island. Chuck and me shelling peas. A lineup photo of all five of us children. Another of the dogs.

"But what about Sylvester?" I blurted out, suddenly not sure Mama knew how much Amelia had loved her own son. "And Perry Lee, her nephew?"

Mama looked at me, and pushed my bangs back from my forehead. "I've put Sylvester's picture in her hand," she answered, "next to her heart."

Thank you. And it was then that it started feeling real, the loss and the permanence. It was then that my tears started with such abundance that they drowned the searing numbness, clenched my stomach, pushed against my throat, and pooled in my eyes until they could only flow over as there was nowhere else to hide. *Mimi*.

Mama retrieved the small black prayer book Amelia had taken with her to church every Sunday from a deeper fold in her bag. "And I have Sylvester's spelling book," she said, showing us the fragile book. "And a letter I found from Perry Lee."

I nodded. But Chuck was still silent.

"You want me to do it?" Mama whispered to him. "I can put it all under her pillow or down by her side."

Chuck looked up at Mama's face like he'd never seen her before. "Don't you want her to remember you, too?" he asked in a hoarse, bitter whisper.

Mama sank against the hard wooden back of the pew.

"I don't believe it's what Amelia would want," she sighed.

And with those words, I realized that all my vague thoughts that something was wrong between Mama and Amelia had been justified, and that Chuck had perhaps always known. Chuck, at age nine, had perhaps known more about Amelia's life than I did or ever would. He had recognized what it meant that Amelia was my mother's employee, that Amelia wasn't really part of the family, and that while she may have loved us in a way, she didn't love us, nor did my mother love her, like family. And it was in that moment that Chuck stopped being the baby of the family. It was in that moment that I understood why Amelia seemed to love him more—he was the baby, the innocent. My newly formed tears silently dripped onto my lap, creating a wet spot on the dress I hadn't worn in months, a dress Amelia had ironed.

Chuck scooted to the other side of the pew, away from both Mama and me. I knew that he had lost more than I had lost. He had loved her unconditionally, while I'd asked her for a love she could not give. I'd asked her to love me like her own child, which of course she could never do, and Chuck must have seen this. He'd seen it and had never asked the same. He'd seen it and loved her more fiercely. And she'd gloried in his love, let her heart fill, and kept him next to her, both of them understanding what I did not, that in the asking is the taking.

The next day, I stood at Amelia's grave, feeling broken but with a promise not to forget her. Chuck was dry eyed. My eleven-year-old heart knew we would never be the same. I looked away and stared as the six pallbearers lowered Amelia into her grave—six young black men, including the twins I'd briefly met once behind Aunt Carrie's house, all dressed in matching coats and ties. I couldn't remember the words that were spoken, but could never forget the handfuls of earth thrown on her casket. Nor would I forget seeing the man in overalls smoking a cigarette as he sat on a bulldozer parked behind a tree. He was waiting to push dirt over her as the Reverend Cook blessed her passing. *I won't forget you, Mimi.*

Epilogue

MY MOTHER PROMISED we would buy a headstone, but we never did. My father decided the two hundred dollars—an amount that would have taken Amelia years to accumulate, that she had left specifically for Chuck's education in her one-paragraph will—was better used for other things.

Chuck, now in his fifties, races from one part of the world to another, and doesn't for a moment sit closely to anyone. My other brother and sisters have scattered to different parts of the country.

The night before I was married, Amelia visited me in my dreams and said I didn't need her anymore. She was wrong. I've kept her with me throughout so many decisions, decisions about how I wanted to live and what I taught my children. They, too, are grown now, and I have told them these stories and have shown them the church where Amelia was buried. Yet I remain haunted by how little I truly know of Amelia's life, of her history, of her true feelings. I can't and won't forget her, but wonder if I have given her description so that I can define myself—still asking her to give me more than I can give back.

I can still feel the warmth of her hand tightly gripping mine as I leaned back to look over at Chuck on the other side of her huge hips, his own hand held with equal determination. She cared for us in more ways than I can know, but not as I'd imagined as a young child.

Amelia MacIntosh was the last of thirteen children to be born to an unknown mother in North Carolina in 1902. She married Peter MacIntosh in 1916—a man who worked for the railroad, had syphilis, and may have seen a doctor at Tuskegee. In 1920, she gave birth to one child, Sylvester, who preceded her in death from pneumonia in 1932. She devoted herself to the Lord, and in 1959 her job moved her to New Jersey where she remained until she died of complications caused by syphilis in April of 1964. She lies alone, in a plot surrounded by strangers, in an unmarked grave.

The Civil Rights Bill of 1964 was passed two months after her death.

Acknowledgments

My sisters read and reread the manuscript, each offering suggestions that helped provide the most accurate portrayal of the people and the times of my childhood. My mother gave her full support when I asked her permission to make the story public. To all three, I give my thanks and my love.

I would also like to thank Amy Quale, my editor at Wise Ink, and Harry Quarles. Their help and encouragement has been immeasurable.

Reader's Guide

Small Moments illustrates many social issues seen throughout American history. These issues include racism, sexism, classism, and addiction. Mary M. Barrow also addresses many of these issues on her website. You can find it at marymillsbarrowbooks.com.

Author Q & A

How do you define "creative nonfiction," and why did you choose the genre to write *Small Moments*?

The term "creative nonfiction" means sticking to the truth as much as possible. The stories are true, the characters are real people, and the places are real. However, elements used in the craft of fiction are introduced to create cohesion and to introduce ideas.

Small Moments was a progression of different approaches. At first, I simply wrote as many stories as I could remember about Amelia. This was an interesting exercise in memory, but the only cohesive element was that the focus was on her. Then I decided that I would rewrite some of these same stories with a view to explore how Amelia affected me as a child and as the person I became. The more that I thought about it, the more I realized how closely her experience paralleled what was happening in the country. At that point, writing the book became easy. I had the thread that I needed to tie the stories together.

If I had been writing pure memoir, I would not have been able to explore the essence of her experience, as I was too young at the time to recognize what it represented. The events I write about are as close to factual as memories a very young mind will allow. It was interesting to compare those memories to the memories my family had of the same events.

I am a private person so it was not easy for me to publicly relive some of the more difficult parts of my childhood. However, if these stories, or "small moments," help to illustrate a different time and an extraordinary person, it is worth the effort.

When you sat down to write the story of your childhood, how were you affected? What was it like stepping into your child-self as a character? What was it like reliving Amelia's story as your adult self?

This wasn't easy to write. I was concerned about getting the facts right and about the responses of my family. But it's done. It took fifty years to finally fulfill my graveside promise to Amelia, and in doing so, my memory of her is more alive than ever.

How does *Small Moments* show that racism hurts white people?

In the story of my childhood, racism hurt; it stole my innocence and replaced it with a deep sense of sorrow, mistrust, and alienation. Amelia's life seemed endlessly sad, though I did not understand at the time how much of her pain was caused by racism (as became obvious later). I felt helplessness in being unable to make changes; anger at the injustice; guilt for being part of the problem; and resentment and mistrustfulness toward those people who were in positions of authority but not making changes—teachers, politicians, religious leaders, parents, and neighbors.

My father's racism was overt, which made it easier to reject. However, I don't believe for one moment that his lessons did not have a profound effect on me. Many of my simple, day-to-day decisions raise conflicting questions about whether my motives are based in racism.

Confronting racism helps to establish an honest reality. Hopefully, telling Amelia's story will help me continue to confront the many injustices she experienced.

How is the idea of patriarchy illustrated in *Small Moments*? What impact did paternalism have on Amelia? Could this happen today?

The most obvious answers can be found in the chapter titled "The Bridge." This is the story of when Amelia's husband, Peter, was sent back to Tennessee by my father. I don't know how much choice Amelia had about going with him, if any, but the speed at which Peter was dispatched would not have left any time for her to consider alternatives. I also don't believe she was consulted in the decision to remove Peter from the household.

In retrospect, this feels like the liberties that slave owners had when making decisions about the lives of those in their charge. Was this a lingering bit of entitlement and racism passed down to my father? Or was it his way of "protecting" his family and Amelia? I don't know. I have to believe that he felt he was protecting his children and Amelia from alcoholic related violence. Maybe it was both.

Having said this, my father, like most men in the 1950s and 1960s, expected to be treated as the "master" of the family. Paternalism was the norm. Was he any better or worse in this regard? I don't know. What is important is that in the decades since, the extremely negative effects of paternalism on the lives of women and children have been brought into sharp focus and are debated. There is still a very long way to go, but I am encouraged.

How do the opening historical paragraphs at the beginnings of chapters illuminate the family story?

It's an interesting question; the tiny bits of history that I included at the beginning of chapters were meant to illustrate the restrictions in Amelia's world. They did, of course, spill over into the lives of the children whom she cared for. For example, she was not allowed to sleep in a berth on a Pullman train. Consequently, my brother and I slept with her in a "coloreds-only" passenger car, an experience they were unlikely to have had otherwise.

In the book, the child Mary experiences confusion over the love that is shared between her and Amelia, yet she expresses that Chuck seems to understand it better. As an adult, how do you see that love? Was it mutual?

Amelia's position was, no doubt, complicated. She took care of babies and as they grew older she was not allowed to make any real decision on their behalf nor did the children have any expectation of her beyond simple caregiving. Babies and the youngest children must have been the easiest for her to give affection, as they did not question why she could not give more. Further, Amelia had lost a son and she was growing old. Chuck, a boy, maybe seemed like her last opportunity to feel any of the maternal bond she'd felt for her own son. I think Amelia loved me just as she loved all of us; it was a limited kind of love that was doomed to fade and she knew that.

I think it is a terrible mistake when people say the men and women who worked for them and maybe lived with them as part of their job were "just like family." It is simply not true, and making such a statement can only be seen as a means to justify or cover oppressive behavior. Somehow, I think Chuck intuitively understood this and so his relationship with Amelia was more honest.

Book Group Discussion Questions

How was Amelia regarded differently in New Jersey as opposed to Tennessee?

How does the story show that racism hurts all people? Some examples?

How would physical punishment by parents have been regarded at the time of the story? Now?

How did the civil rights movement change things for those in similar situations to Amelia's?

What did Mary mean when she said either she or her father had to disappear? (Answer provided at www.marymillsbarrowbooks.com.)

Give some examples of how Amelia sustained the family, beyond cooking and cleaning. What sustained Amelia?

How would society be today had the civil rights movement not occurred?

Can you think of similar events to the Tuskeegee experiment that have occurred in history?

How would, or could, Amelia negotiate a raise for her services? What alternatives were available to Amelia if she had been unwilling to tolerate her circumstances? What better course of life would have been open to Amelia at the time of the story? Now?

How do you view the mother's relationship with Amelia?

Were the father's negative attitudes purely racist? What other attitudes did he demonstrate?

What part did Amelia's church play in her experience in New England? What does it show about the role of African American churches in the civil rights movement?

How is classism seen among whites in the story? Blacks?

Did Northerners tend to view unfavorable race relations as a problem mainly existing in the South? Why do you suppose that is?

How would you have behaved as one of these family members? How did the feelings (love) of these family members toward Amelia differ from their feelings (love) for each other?

How was alcohol depicted in the stories? What does the story suggest about the ways alcohol affects families? How did it affect this family?

Are race relations better today? If so, how? If not, what can be done?